Editorial Briefs

What do you know, it's happened. People said this magazine would never last a year, but here we are! It's been an interesting year filled with the standard ups-and-downs of finding our way, but as we bring out issue number four, Sam and I are practically bursting with joy as we reach this pinnacle achievement.

Wondering why we're so pleased? Let's start with the obvious. We've reconstructed the magazine for our final time to bring you the very best format possible. We're introducing quite a few new programs, but I'll let Sam fill you in on those. After all, it's only fair that we both get to talk about all of the new and fabulous developments. So let me see, what fun parts will I tell you about…

I think I'll start with the exciting news that as of this issue and all of those to come, Autograph Quarterly will be available for purchase through Amazon, Barnes & Noble, and a host of other distribution outlets! Back issues of the magazine will also be made available on Amazon over the course of the next few weeks. They won't include the limited pieces donated to us for our subscribers by Star Wares, but collectors should enjoy the ability to have spares if they need them.

Our 2012 issues are going to filled with new features that will hopefully be items that collectors all over the world will find appealing. Starting with Volume Two, Issue One (how I love the sound of that), there will be a quarterly schedule of signing events from all over the world. This will include everything from celebrity autograph conventions to sports memorabilia signing events to book signings. It's one way we're going to help collectors add to their archives with absolutely authentic items. What could be better than standing in front of your favorites while they sign a new treasure for you?

We're bringing back the autograph exemplar section that we had in our premiere issue but instead of a few signatures, we'll include at least three pages of autographs in each issue. That way, you can view and compare the signatures of the stars to your collection. Can't ever tell, study them hard enough and you may learn a little something along the way too!

Perhaps the news that is making me downright giddy with anticipation is an idea that popped into my mind a few weeks ago. I've been contacted with so many wonderful story ideas from assorted authors that I took the idea to Sam, who promptly shared my enthusiasm, so without further adieu, it's my pleasure to announce that twice per year there will be specialized supplimental issues of Autograph Quarterly. The Spring supplement will be all about the Entertainment Industry and will feature stories and illustrations about Hollywood's biggest and brightest stars. The Fall suppliment will be centered around the Sports Industry and will cover any and every sport writers wish to cover. Those issues will be exclusively available through Amazon and AQ only, so I'll keep you up to date on their progress. The beautiful part is that we're not locked in, so the 2013 issues can cover History and Transportation for collectors in those fields. The possibilities are endless!

I realize I'm a bit long-winded in this issue, but bear with me because I'm almost finished. As we come to the end of our first year in publication, I'd like to take a moment to thank those who have given their time and talent to helping create a publication that we can all be proud of. It's been a pleasure to work with each of you and I'm looking forward to doing so for quite a few years to come. To our advertisers – Thank you for believing in Autograph Quarterly and for helping allow us to bring entertaining and educational articles to collectors from around the world. We couldn't have done it without you!

Until next time…

Victoria Gregory
Editor-in-Chief

The Publisher's View

Welcome to another edition of Autograph Quarterly! We are happy you're a subscriber and with the introduction of our new programs, you will be pretty happy about it too!

Many of you may have already heard about the new Autograph Quarterly Seal of Approval program, which we're in the process of instituting with the help of over twenty recognized experts in autograph authentication in fields such as Entertainment, Presidential, Historical, Sports, and much more. These experts, along with us at the magazine, feel it's time to try reclaiming some sanity in our hobby, and we're starting with making eBay more accountable for the millions of forgeries they sell in our category.

How are we going to do this? Simple! In the coming months we will be awarding our AQ Seal of Approval to dealers in autographs on eBay and other online sales places. They will be able to display the seal only if the 20 plus experts helping us agree that they predominently sell authentic material and have a way to be easily reached in the event of a customer complaint. They must hand sign their own COA's guaranteeing the items they sell and stand behind refunding a person's purchase should an item be proven to not be authentic.

We know that no one is 100% all the time. No one. All dealers have made mistakes at one time or another, but like a good doctor, you want someone to buy from who is reputable and doing the best they can and stands behind any mistakes they make. The Seal of Approval will show that the dealer displaying it has had his inventory vetted by experts and peers. Those experts will re-inspect the dealer's inventory every six months after a seal is given and we shall have the sole right to remove a seal should a complaint come to us that the dealer has not handled in a timely manner, or should their inventory no longer represent predominently authentic material. You, as a collector, should say to a dealer, "No seal? No deal!" and keep your hard earned money to spend with those displaying the seal.

In addition, starting with our next issue, we are offering our subscribers five free authentication opinions per month! A minimum of four experts will look at any item you submit to us here at Autograph Quarterly by e-mailing us with an eBay item number with no less than 48 hours left in the auction. We'll pass it along to our expert panel and you'll receive an answer regarding its authenticity before the end of the auction. If for some reason our experts are inconclusive on the item, they'll tell you why their opinion is inconclusive so you can make an informed decision before buying a piece.

Every month, you'll get five free opinions on items from the experts because after all, shouldn't opinions be free? Why pay for an opinion when it won't help you get a refund, isn't backed up in court, and isn't even signed by one person taking responsibility for it?

Autograph Quarterly will have experts known in the field of the item submitted look at your prospective purchase and even explain to you why an item is or isn't authentic!

Now about the magazine... As you can see, we have gone to the extra expense of square binding it for two reasons. First, the page count is so meaty that it will help the magazine last, and secondly, so many of you are saving your copies (which is what we'd hoped you'd do) that we thought it should be something to sit on your shelves as reference guides!

We have several more significant anoucements to make shortly so stay tuned, and for a list of Seal of Approval Dealers wait for the next issue of AQ, check the website over the coming months, or look for the seal on their listings and if they don't have one, ask them why not? Dealers wishing to diplay the seal can contact us to expedite our experts looking over your inventory.

We are determined to take the hobby back to the place where it was fun, educational, and profitable for everyone. Are you with us? Of course you are!

In the words of Stan Lee: Excelsior!

Samuel Xidas
Publisher

Richard MacCallum

~ Chicago ~

Fine Autographs Since 1972
866 Auburn Court • Highland Park, Illinois 60035
(847) 432-7942 Phone • (847) 432-8685 Fax 24 Hours
0798-922-0386 • London, England

~ London ~

The Autographs: The following presentations are vintage signatures that in most cases have been removed from old autograph albums, letters, documents, etc. and have been mounted under a photograph. Most photos used are approximately 8x10 in size. They are double matted most often in black and white, or other colors that work best with that style of photograph. Most photos are black and white. Most overall sizes are approximately 12x17. Snapshots of these pieces, as well as photocopies of the signatures are available. I carry signatures from all areas of history (and have so since 1972). The items listed below are other autographs available. Some are matted with a photo, some are signed photos, and some are just signatures only.
Call for more details. Foreign orders always welcome.

Walt Disney - $1,495.00

Cary Grant - $295.00

Marilyn Monroe & Joe
DiMaggio - $2,995.00

Walt Disney - $1,495.00
Marlene Dietrich - $195.00
"Houdini" - $795.00
Douglas Fairbanks Sr. - $250.00
Cecil B. DeMille - $195.00
Mother Teresa - $425.00
Henry Fonda - $250.00
Jimi Hendrix - $1,495.00
George Burns - $125.00
George Reeves - $695.00
Colin Clive - $595.00
Liberace (with Piano
   Drawing) - $295.00
Buddy Holly - $795.00
Lupe Velez - $225.00
Margaret Hamilton - $250.00
"Dr. Seuss" (Theodor Seuss
   Geisel) - $395.00
Rockey Marciano - $450.00
Marilyn Monroe - $2,495.00
Frank Lloyd Wright - $595.00
"Laurel & Hardy" - $895.00
Helen Hayes - $125.00
Michael Jackson - $325.00
Lon Chaney Sr. - $795.00
Clark Gable & Vivien
   Leigh - $595.00
Amelia Earhart - $625.00
Ernest Hemingway - $3,150.00
Edward G. Robinson - $250.00
Carole Lombard - $275.00
"The Blues Brothers" - $495.00
Grace Kelly - $395.00
The "Apollo XI Crew" - $2,595.00
U.S. Grant - $595.00
Basil Rathbone - $295.00
Mary Astor - $250.00
Geronimo - $8,595.00
Gary Cooper - $250.00
Cary Grant - $295.00
Casey Stengel - $495.00
W.C. Fields - $395.00
Jimmy Stewart &
   Donna Reed - $325.00
Jimmy Stewart - $125.00
Jimmy Stewart &
   June Allyson - $195.00
Jimmy Stewart &
   Maureen O'Hara - $195.00
Jimmy Stewart &
   Frank Capra - $295.00
Jimmy Stewart &
   Marlene Dietrich - $350.00

James Dean - $2,295.00
"The Maltese Falcon" - $2,195.00
Steve McQueen - $695.00
Sigmund Freud - $1,295.00
Martin Luther King Jr. -
   $2,195.00
"The Wizard of Oz" - $2,195.00
Oscar Wilde - $995.00
Judy Garland - $395.00
Frederic Remington - $525.00
Charles M. Russell - $495.00
James Dean & Sal Mineo
   (on same page) - $2,995.00
Natalie Wood - $295.00
Frank Sinatra - $395.00
Gerald R. Ford - $295.00
Maxfield Parish - $295.00
Alberto Vargas - $425.00
Salvador Dali - $395.00
Erte - $250.00
Marc Chagall - $450.00
Andy Warhol - $425.00
Katharine Hepburn - $275.00
Alfred Hitchcock - $895.00
Rita Hayworth - $225.00
Edgar Allan Poe - $7,995.00
Harold Lloyd - $325.00
Will Rogers - $595.00
Wiley Post - $250.00
Lech Walesa - $295.00
Mary Pickford - $225.00
Charles A. Comiskey - $650.00
John, Lionel and Ethel
   Barrymore - $595.00
John Phillip Sousa - $350.00
Samual Goldwyn - $225.00
Louis B. Mayer - $250.00
Eddie "Rochester"
   Anderson - $195.00
Kurt Vonnegut - $150.00
Marilyn Monroe &
   Joe DiMaggio - $2,995.00
Claudette Colbert - $150.00
"The DiMaggio
   Brothers" - $1,295.00
Clayton Moore - $125.00
Eubie Blake - $150.00
Joe DiMaggio (Signed
   Baseball) - $695.00
Ted Williams (Signed
   Baseball) - $595.00
Mickey Mantle (Signed
   Baseball) - $695.00

Mark Twain - $1,195.00
Walter Huston - $175.00
Ty Cobb - $795.00
Charles Laughton - $195.00
Hal Roach - $195.00
"Gilligan's Island" Cast
   Photo (All 7) - $695.00
Spencer Tracy - $275.00
Jim Morrison - $695.00
Jerry Garcia - $295.00
Ronald Reagan - $395.00
Connie Mack - $695.00
Duke Ellington - $295.00
James Cagney - $175.00
James Cagney &
   Corinne Calvet - $225.00
Bud Abbott & Lou
   Costello - $695.00
Tallulah Bankhead - $175.00
Brigitte Bardot - $125.00
Enrico Caruso - $275.00
Lillian Gish - $125.00
Alger Hiss - $295.00
Bela Lugosi - $595.00
Truman Capote - $225.00
"The Marx Brothers" - $1,395.00
Fay Wray - $175.00
"The Three Stooges" Moe,
   Curley (first names), Larry
   (full name) - $1,495.00
Lucille Ball & Desi Arnaz
   (Full Names) - $595.00
Menachem Begin - $395.00
Yul Brynner - $195.00
Shirley Temple - $295.00
Charles Bronson - $150.00
Madonna (Nude) - $275.00
Margaret Thatcher - $295.00
Peter Lorre - $275.00
Muhammad Ali - $225.00
Roland Winters "Charlie
   Chan" - $125.00
Fred Astaire &
   Ginger Rogers - $395.00
Ronald Coleman - $175.00
Eric Clapton - $75.00
Linus Pauling - $175.00
Humphrey Bogart - $695.00
Boris Karloff - $2,250.00
"Father Knows Best" Cast
   Photo (all 5) - $495.00
Buck Jones - $295.00
John F. Kennedy - $1,895.00

James Dean - $2,295.00

Buddy Holly - $795.00

Lucille Ball &
Desi Arnaz - $595.00

Boris Karloff - $2,250.00

John Wayne - $1,195.00

"The DiMaggio Brothers"
Vince - Joe - Dom - $1,295.00

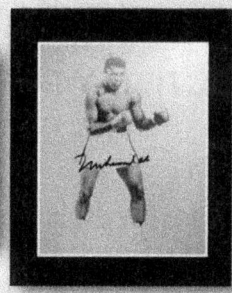

Muhammad Ali (1963) -
$225.00

Ernest Hemingway -
$3,150.00

Stephen Koschal
Autographs, Signed Books, Authentications

Established in 1967, we have supplied libraries, universities, museums, collectors and dealers worldwide. We have been one of the leading advocates of autograph education and are responsible for creating and maintaining possibly the largest autograph reference library in the hobby. We pioneered the establishment of the first fourteen autograph educational courses, of which we instructed two of them.

Our educational writings on the subject of autograph collecting can be found in every autograph trade publication as well as the publications of every major autograph organization.

We offer only genuine autographs in all fields of collecting and in all price ranges.

Our reference books are sought by all those who have an interest in education themselves on collecting autographs. Reference books available, shipping additional:

Gerald R. Ford Autograph Study by Stephen Koschal...$7.50

Robert F. Kennedy Autograph Study by TerMolin, Keyes, Koschal..$20.00

Tiger Woods Signature Study by Stephen Koschal and Todd Mueller..$1.95

Thomas Jefferson's Invisible Hand by Stephen Koschal and Andreas Wiemer...........................$10.00

The Collector's Guide to Muhammad Ali Autographs by Shawn Anderson, Markus Brandes, and Stephen Koschal...$15.00

Ronald Reagan and Nelle Reagan Autograph Mystery Uncovered by Patricia Claren, Stephen Koschal, and Ron Werntz...$10.00

The History of Collecting Executive Mansion, White House, and The White House Cards Signed by the Presidents and their First Ladies by Lynne E. Keyes and Stephen Koschal.........................$20.00

Presidents of the United States Autopen Guide by Stephen Koschal and Andreas Wiemer........$15.00

Stephen Koschal's authentication service is utilized by collectors worldwide, and by dealers, auction houses, and by other authentication services.   Occasional catalogs issued.

ACTIVELY PURCHASING AUTOGRAPH COLLECTIONS
Immediate Payment

Stephen Koschal
P.O. Box 311061
Miami, FL 33231 USA

Phone: 561-315-3622
E-Mail: skoschal@aol.com
Website: www.stephenkoschal.com

INSIDE THIS ISSUE

COMING IN 2012!

Autograph Dealer
Seal of Approval

Selected as a
premier dealer by
the Autograph
Quarterly Team of Experts

2012

Buyers: look for this seal to be assured what you're buying is real!
Dealers: contact us to apply for your seal today!

Autograph Quarterly

PUBLISHER
S. Eugene Xidas
samxidas@autographquarterly.com

EDITOR-IN-CHIEF
Victoria Gregory
victoriagregory@autographquarterly.com

ASSISTANT TO PUBLISHER
Tiffany Kasey

ASSISTANT TO EDITOR
Christine McDermott

CONTRIBUTORS

Richard Altman, Brian Green, Stephen Koschal, Todd Mueller, Dr. Zoltan Marian, Nelson Deedle and Patricia Claren

Questions about Autograph Quarterly?
questions@autographquarterly.com

Autograph Quarterly welcomes collecting enthusiasts and dealers alike to submit articles for inclusion in upcoming issues. If you'd like to have an article considered, please e-mail it to either the publisher or editor. If you'd prefer to mail in your submission, or if you have a book on the hobby you'd like to have reviewed, please send it to the address listed below. We will contact you to let you know if your submission has been accepted for publication.

Please note that all articles submitted become the property of Autograph Quarterly and cannot be released for inclusion in any other publication.

Advertising inquiries should be directed to Victoria Gregory.

Subscribe online at www.autographquarterly.com

Autograph Quarterly
29910 Murrieta Hot Springs Road, Suite G, PMB 338
Murrieta, CA 92562
(702) 354-3685

The Many Signatures of Lady Gaga

By Nelson Deedle

I am often asked by collectors about the challenge of adding an authentic Lady Gaga autograph to their collection. Her autograph is very sought after and as varied as her outfits.

It is not impossible to meet Lady Gaga. In fact, compared to other stars in the prime of their career like Madonna, Whitney Houston and Cher, she is easy to meet. Gaga is fan friendly and always makes time to meet with fans around scheduled events. On a recent radio show appearance in Los Angeles, she stopped the limo and announced that she had exactly 23 minutes to sign autographs, and that she did! Most fans left with multiples. While on the same publicity tour she stayed at the Chateau Marmont in Hollywood. She routinely signed for the crowd coming and going from the hotel.

One of the best ways to get an autograph from a contemporary music artist, such as Lady Gaga, is to join their fan club. As a fan club member you will be offered prime seats, meet 'n' greet opportunities, and merchandise that will not be available to the general public. Although the rules state that the artist will sign ONLY 1 AUTOGRAPH per fan, you can normally get 3-4 items signed, which more than pays for the price of the meet 'n' greet. Also, as a rule, meet 'n' greet photo-ops are much better than anything you could possibly get by asking in a crowd on the street.

If you aren't lucky enough to meet Gaga, you can look to the marketplace. There are numerous styles of Gaga's autograph that you will find for sale. After you find the Gaga autograph that you want to buy, how can you do your due diligence to know that it is 100% authentic? The answer is: you can't. Sadly, she has so many versions of her autograph that it's nearly impossible. Buying an authentic Gaga autograph is an instance where a solid relationship with a well known dealer is key. As with most contemporary autographs, the chain of providence is short and in many cases can be easily traced.

I have seen some general consistencies that might help you in your quest for an authentic Lady Gaga autograph.

1: First known version of Gaga's signature. Signed in 2008 it shows the formation of every letter in 'Lady' and almost every letter in 'Gaga.'

2: The second consistent version of Gaga's signature is full of swirls and looks like is it signed haphazardly.

3: The third and most short lived of Gaga's signature. The "L" resemblances a lighting bolt.

4: A shortened version of illustration 3.

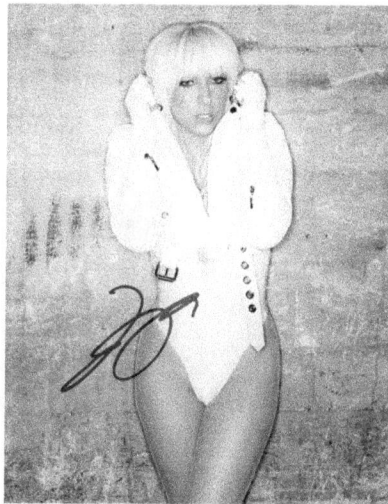

5 & 6: These photos were signed less than a minute apart. Gaga was sitting down and had ample time to inscribe each photo. Notice how the two signature don't resemble each other.

7- 10: These three illustration represent the fourth, and by far, the most consistent autograph of Gaga. Gaga signs this version of her autograph on most occasions.

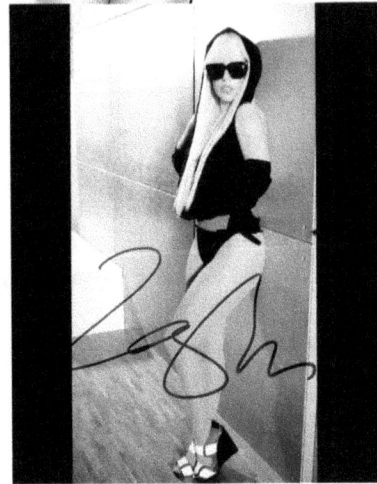

11: Slight variation adding a heart at the beginning of her signature.

12: A rare look at Gaga's writing. This letter was addressed to fans in Los Angeles in 2011. Notice how the "L" in Little is very similar to her "L" in the majority of signed photos illustrated.

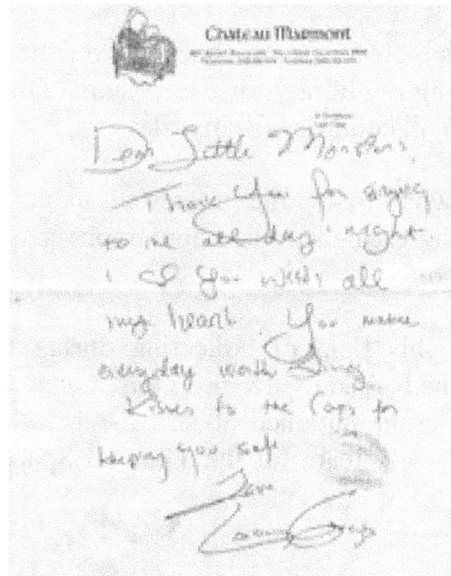

13: A closeup of the signature on the letter bears no resemblance to any of the signed photos.

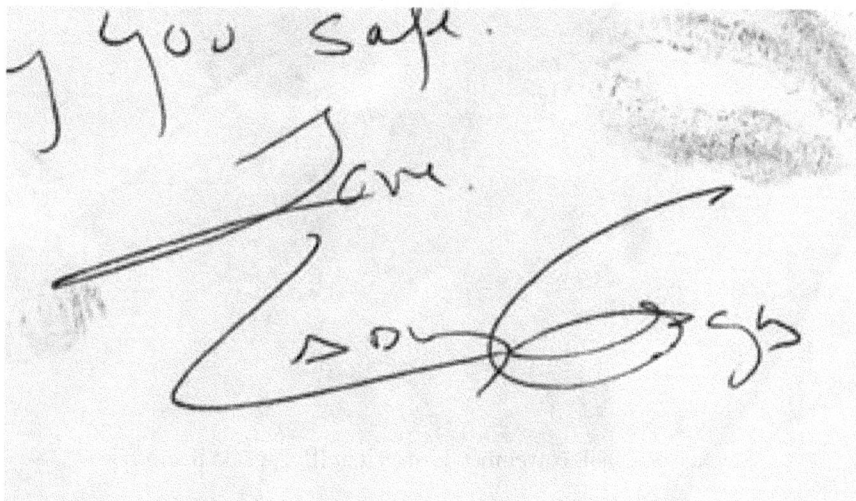

Apollo XI: One Source of the Signed Photographs

By Stephen Koschal

Those who visit my office always seem shocked over the size of my reference files. After all, I have been building my library for many years. One large file I have is on the astronauts. Astronauts from all countries fill my files.

I was recently asked what made me interested in collecting the autographs of astronauts. Actually, my interest in astronaut autographs is mostly limited to those men who have walked on the moon.

I became interested in this field of collecting during the early 1950s and read everything I could find on the Russian space program. Later, in the mid to late 60s, I was part of the U.S. Space program stationed aboard the U.S.S. Aucilla (AO-56). I was involved in the capsule recovery team for the Titan III Space Shot between Brazil and Africa.

Stephen Koschal, November 1966, Titan III Capsule Recovery

I am often asked what (in my personal collection) is my favorite astronaut autograph. My favorite is certainly not the most valuable item. Back in the early 1990s, there was a trade publication named Autograph Times. A cartoonist by the name of Bruce Petus would draw a cartoon for the publication. In July 1994, he painted in watercolor, an astronaut on the moon holding an American Flag with the planet Earth in the background. To the right side he drew in ink a portrait of John F. Kennedy. This was published in The News-Sun. Petus mailed his original painting to Neil Armstrong. Armstrong inscribed and dated the piece: "To Bruce, Neil Armstrong, 10-16-94."

- APOLLO 11 - FIRST MAN ON THE MOON -
Original Watercolor by Bruce Petus Signed by Neil Armstrong

It is well accepted by experts of space autographs that Neil Armstrong basically stopped signing autographs in the spring of 1994. After that, most every request was responded to with the standard letter of refusal.

Trouble is the hobby seems to be infested with any 8"x10" photographs signed by Neil Armstrong, Buzz Aldrin, and Michael Collins. Some have sold in the range of $20,000. Unfortunately, many of the photos that appear for sale in antique malls, on the internet, and yes, even with so-called autograph dealers are not genuinely signed by the three astronauts.

"Official NASA Fifth Manned Apollo Crew Photo"

The photo above contains Autopen signatures of the three astronauts. A major source of thousands of these photographs was Marquette University.

On Saturday, November 9, 1969, the three astronauts were present at the University to receive Pere Marquette Discovery Award Medals. James Dickey was present for a special reading of his poem "The Moon Ground."

Persons attending this event received a beautiful presentation folder made of imitation blue leather. It had an embossed gold seal of Marquette University on the cover.

Marquette University Presentation Folder

On the inside cover was a printed description of the event. Named The Pere Marquette Discovery Award Dinner and held Saturday, November 8, 1969 at Brooks Memorial Union, Marquette University, Milwaukee, Wisconsin.

Description of the Event

On the second panel laid over gold colored silk is the Official NASA Signed Photograph. These presentation folders are sometimes sold intact. Most of the time, the photo has been removed from the folder and sold to an uneducated collector.

Should readers of Autograph Quarterly have in their collection a similar photo signed by the three Apollo XI astronauts, it may be in your best interest to make sure the signatures on your photo does not match the ones illustrated above.

Francisco, One of Modern America's Greatest Sculptors

By Patricia Claren

Try to name a single person who wouldn't want a signature of Michelangelo in their collection of autographs?

Among other works, Michelangelo (1475-1564) is known for his Pieta at St. Peter's Basilica and he is responsible for the painting of the ceiling in the Sistine Chapel in Vatican City. However, he may best be known for his seventeen foot Statue of David. The standing male nude was to represent the Biblical hero David. The statue was sculpted from a six ton block of marble found in the quarries at Carrara in the northern region of Tuscany. Just a few months ago I traveled through this region and was amazed to see all the quarries still very active in the marble white mountains of this region.

Originally, a Florentine sculptor by the name of Agostino di Duccio was contracted to create David. In 1464, Agostino began to shape the legs, feet and torso. For reasons unknown, the project came to a halt. Ten years later, Antonio Rossellino was commissioned to take up where Agostino left off. But the contract was soon terminated and the block of marble was neglected for the next twenty-five years.

Only twenty-six years old, Michelangelo convinced the Operai that he deserved the commission to complete the unfinished project. He began work in the summer of 1501 and the statue was completed in 1504. It took four days to move the statue one half mile from Michelangelo's workshop to the Piazza della Signoria, a square in front of City Hall in Florence, Italy. To protect it from damage, it was removed from the Piazza and is displayed in its currrent location in the Accademia Gallery, also in Florence.

Can you imagine a collector meeting Michelangelo and requesting a piece of marble chopped away from the six ton block that would end up being the statue of David? Better yet, imagine asking Michelangelo to autograph the fragment?

MICHELANGELO (BUONARROTI), 1475-1564. Italian painter, sculptor, architect and poet. A major figure of the Renaissance and one of the greatest names in the history of art. His major sculptures include David in Florence and Pieta at St Peter's, Rome. He was responsible for the decoration in fresco style of the ceiling of the Sistine Chapel in the Vatican. A form of his autograph and a rare ALS. (The British Library.)

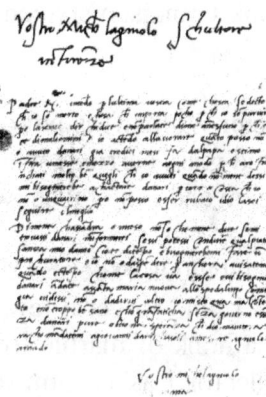

Signature of Michelangelo

In November 1987, Robert Batchelder offered a one page document in the hand of Michelangelo but not signed. It was simply a financial document and it was priced at $75,000.

Francisco Sotomayor, born in the year 1956, is an American artist and sculptor who currently resides in Colorado. He is of Puerto Rican decent and claims he may have ties to one of our Supreme Court Judges.

Known simply as Francisco, he is the creator of the world famous sculpture "American Woman."

Signed portrait of "American Woman"

This marble statue depicts a life size woman wearing an evening gown, holding a rose, reclining on top of a ten foot long concert grand piano. It is the first ever marble sculpture in history to have protruding eyelashes.

Francisco is a self taught artist. In 2001 he began the "American Woman" project. Out of a composite of six models, taking the best feature out of each woman, he was able to make his completed work unique. The woman and piano were sculpted out of a single twenty one ton block of Colorado Yule (Valley Gold Vein) marble. This work of art measures 124 inches by 62 inches by 84 inches and weighs a whopping ten thousand pounds. Working alone, it took Francisco sixteen hundred hours within a little over a two year period to finish.

The statue of the "American Woman" is not on permanent display. Francisco displays this beauty in a large protected glass carriage which can be towed to various conventions, exhibit halls and numerous gem and mineral shows throughout the United States.

Meeting Francisco was a fabulous experience. He is quite friendly and generous with his autograph. Not only was I able to get a few different signed portraits of "American Woman" I was graced with a hunk of marble from the original six ton block. Of course being an avid autograph collector I asked him to autograph the block. Now this signed chunk of white marble is one of my favorite pieces in my personal collection of autographs.

Francisco with Pat Claren in front of "American Woman"

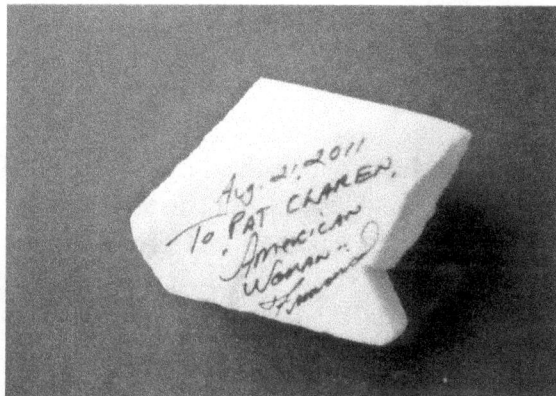

Chunk of marble from the original block inscribed and signed by Francisco

Francisco's oil paintings and pencil drawings, many done as studies for sculptures, also display a realism of the human experience.

Find out the schedule of the "American Woman" and it will be well worth your while to see it in person. A bonus of course would be meeting Francisco and getting his autograph. Francisco has been compared to the Italian Renaissance sculptor and painter Michelangelo.

The Man Who Created 007...

By Richard E. Altman

No, *not* Ian Fleming. Fleming created the character all right, though where he got the double-0-seven designation has been an object of speculation for more than a half century, with no definitive (or at least verifiable) answer ever provided.

How Fleming came up with James Bond's "007" classification may be in doubt but there can be no doubt that it has become one of the world's most iconic and identifiable brands...And like Coca Cola and Nike and even Superman's diamond shaped "S" shield, the *"007"* with the gun barrel extending from the seven is of one the world's most identifiable brand logos and 'brand extensions.'

Ironically, it may be the only major brand in the world that attracts *other* major brands to it, in hopes that the 007 allure will rub off by association. Long before motion picture "product placements" became a standard practice, Bond appeal began attaching itself to "007" products of every description.

Soon, established brands – perhaps noting the success Aston Martin automobiles was having with its association with the super spy franchise – began seeking ways of placing the 007 logo alongside of their own on "special" and "limited edition" products.

In virtually every case the coveted logo features the iconic three digits with a gun barrel extending off the third.

Created in 1962, the logo was originally intended for use on a publicity release sheet sent to movie exhibitors by United Artists to tout one of its upcoming releases, "Dr No." The logo design was soon applied to the lobby posters and advertisements for that movie and in some form, every other official Bond movie since.

The man who created that logo was a freelance commercial artist named Joseph Caroff. Called in by renowned United Artists Creative Director David Chasman, Caroff was asked if he knew of Ian Fleming's James Bond books.

Original 007 logo circa 1962, signed by artist Joseph Caroff, October 13, 2011

"I *was* familiar with the books...*I was a fan*," Caroff recalled recently. "Chasman explained the assignment to me off I went. When I first looked at the 007, I saw the stem of the seven as the handle of the gun. It took me about six seconds to come up with the concept and maybe five or six hours to come up with actual art.

"I knew that the gun Bond used was a PK Walther, so I went to the library to see what it looked like. It was just a short barrel gun, not very dramatic. So I threw out the Walther research and just created a gun barrel design I thought looked good.

"There was no pre-existing typeface. It was all hand-lettered and drawn,"

Not wishing to take more credit that is his due, Caroff emphasizes that the 007 logo was his only contribution to the "Dr. No" poster art. Indeed, the figural renditions of Sean Connery, cigarette in one hand, silenced Walther PPK in the other and four alluring women in various states of dress and undress were created by artist/illustrator Mitchell Hooks. Subsequent poster artists include Boris Grinsson, Frank McCarthy and the legendary Robert McGinnis, but it is Caroff's contribution that extends across all 23-franchise Bond pictures.

Original movie poster for "Dr. No" (1962) with Caroff's 007 logo employed twice in the design. Signed by Joseph Caroff, October 13, 2011

Looking at some of the more modern renditions of the logo, Caroff misses the strong clean lines of his original. The gun barrel details have changed, the typography varied a bit over the years, but the logo concept remains 100% Caroff.

"I got paid $300 for that logo," revealed Caroff. That was the going rate for a publicity release sheet in those days."

While the final artwork for Caroff's 007 may still live in a United Artists file somewhere, none of the original preliminary sketches, artwork or ad comps Caroff did for the 007 logo survive.

"I'm not a very good collector...my friends give me a hard time about all the time."

Caroff's work for Chasman and United Artists did not begin with the 007 logo. Indeed, Caroff's iconic poster design for the film version of "West Side Story" (often erroneously attributed to graphic artist giant Saul Bass) preceded Caroff's 007 assignment.

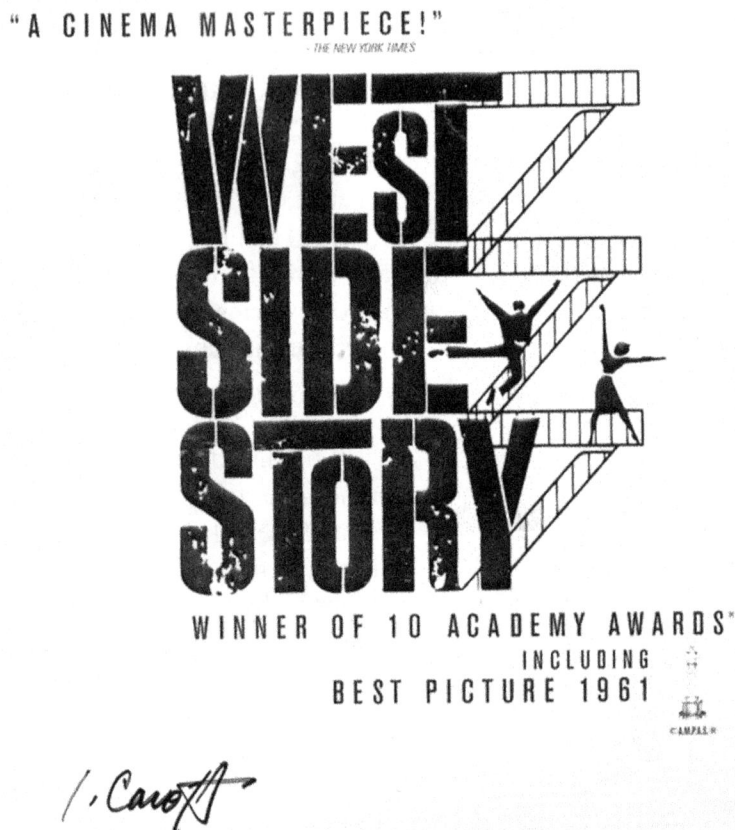

Original movie poster art for "West Side Story" (1961) created by artist Joseph Caroff and often erroneously credited to Saul Bass. Signed by Joseph Caroff, October 13, 2011

The years following included creation of movie poster art for such productions as the Beatles "A Hard Day's Night;" the Jane Fonda sci-fi fantasy "Barbarella;" the original French version of "La Cage Aux Folles;" Norman Jewison's original "Rollerball" with James Caan; Bernardo Bertolucci's groundbreaking "Last Tango in Paris," with Marlon Brando; Martin Scorcese's controversial "Last Temptation of Christ" (that actually incorporated Caroff's crown of thorns poster motif into the film's opening credits); Bob Fosse's musical masterpiece "Cabaret" with Liza Minnelli and Joel Grey, and a handful of Woody Allen classics including "Manhattan" and "Zelig."

His logo work had likewise advanced since the early 1960s. Among Caroff's designs are the trademark and opening title animation for Orion pictures; the imprint for ABC News and their news magazine show "20/20," as well as the logo for the network's broadcast of the Olympic Games that intertwined the lowercase abc with the Olympic rings.

Ultimately Caroff started his own successful graphics shop, employing dozens or other artists, before retiring and turning his complete attention from commercial art to fine art.

Both a painter and sculptor, Caroff's work often incorporates the two mediums with a healthy dose of wit, irony and (as one of his 1990s artwork collections was named), "the iconic metaphor."

Of those art pieces Caroff observed, "These works have sometimes been called sculptures that have been painted. I think of them as paintings that have a third dimension."

At the conclusion of the art catalog for his "Iconic Metaphor" collection, Caroff poses a question and a stream of possible answers about his ongoing work. *"Why do I do this,"* he asks. *"To fight against the inevitable end of doing? To express something no one has asked me about? To stimulate approval? To evoke regard? To revel in exhibitionism? To bask in the transient glow of recognition? It doesn't matter. Energy for the doing and doubt about motivations are in continual struggle. The doing is what matters. It banishes doubt. Temporarily."*

Recently, Caroff published a collection of remarkably funny, insightful and incisive cartoons on the subject of psychotherapy entitled "all lying down" ('drawn" says the cover, "while sitting up"). As we conclude our meeting I note that his cartoon work seems to be an amalgam of the style and sensibilities of classic *New Yorker* cartoons and the work of Jules Feiffer. I mean it as praise, yet I as I say it I realize that some artists bridle at *any* comparisons.

Responds Caroff simply*: "Thank you...I take that as a compliment."*

The back cover of "all lying down" relates the following:

"Joe Caroff's first book jacket design was for Norman Mailer's "The Naked and the Dead." His first film campaign was for "West Side Story." His first trademark was for Ian Fleming's '007'."

Now, as he approaches his 91st birthday and his 66th year of marriage to his wife Phyllis, Joseph Caroff is preparing for another New York City gallery show of his most recent fine art works.

"The doing is what matters."

Joseph Caroff in his New York City studio, October 13, 2011.

The Screen's First James Bond...

Eight years to the month *before* Sean Connery gazed across the green baize of a casino baccarat table in Dr. No and introduced himself with the now iconic phrase "Bond...James Bond," another actor brought James Bond to the screen at another baccarat table in another Casino.

Admittedly, this first screen portrayal was on the *small* screen as part of a live television anthology series on CBS called "Climax!" The actor who portrayed *American* agent James Bond (more about that later) was Barry Nelson and the script was based on Ian Fleming's recently published first Bond novel "Casino Royale."

Barry Nelson circa 1954 signed, "Best Wishes from the screen's first James Bond Barry Nelson." Signed 2003.

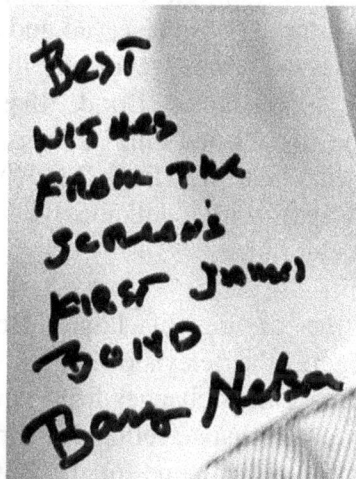

Detail of inscription on the above picture

So it was that on Thursday evening October 21st between 8:30-9:30 PM EST, the CBS Television Network debuted "Casino Royale."

Composite photo of Barry Nelson, Linda Christian and Peter Lorre sent out by CBS publicity department in 1954 promoting CLIMAX! production of "Casino Royale."

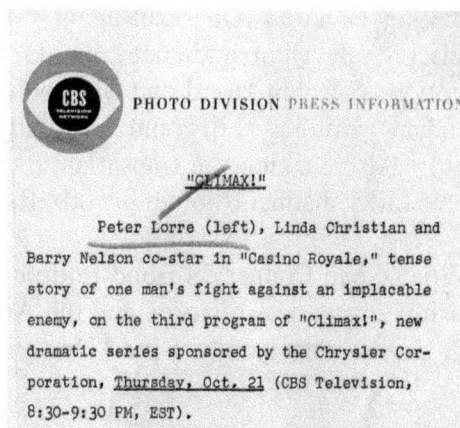

Reverse of composite photo with cutline, providing details of the production.

While some Bond purists may point out that though Barry Nelson's incarnation was the character's first portrayal, it does not technically count as it was live television and not recorded on film. Fact is, "Casino Royale" was indeed captured on film thanks to a pre-cursor to videotape that was routinely used in the 1950's called kinescope. Simply put, a specially designed film camera recorded the live telecast off of an in-studio TV monitor making it truly, the first James Bond film.

Lost and forgotten for years, the kinescope reportedly turned up amidst other cans of film at a flea market in California where it was purchased for a song. When the new owner reviewed the contents of the various film cans he purchased, he discovered that he now owned the original "Casino Royale" kinescope.

Thus an important piece of Bond history – indeed film history – was preserved and an array of new Bond "firsts" revealed. In addition to the screen's first James Bond, there was of necessity, the first "Bond Girl" ably portrayed by Linda Christian and the first Bond Villain, Le Chiffre, played with deliciously understated menace by Peter Lorre.

Beyond the casting of James Bond as an American agent, the television script of "Casino Royale" featured other changes from Ian Fleming's original novel. Perhaps feeling Fleming's choice of Vesper Lynd as the name for the Bond girl was too fanciful, the producers changed her name to

"The Anatomic Bomb": Linda Christian, the first Bond Girl.

Valerie Mathis. Mathis was of course the (male) French secret service agent that assists Bond in the book. And speaking of name and nationality changes, there was a *British* agent assisting the American Bond named Leiter, though the producers inexplicably changed his first name from Felix to Clarence.

Making Bond an American agent was reportedly based on the producers' belief that American television audiences would not accept an English hero (with the possible exception of Robin Hood and Sherlock Holmes). This American Bond does retain his legendary gambling skills (and is actually referred to as "Card Sense Jimmy Bond" in one scene). Also making the transatlantic crossing were Bond's reputation as a ladies man and his killer instinct (though his 00- designation and license to kill is never mentioned).

When Sean Connery's Bond returned to the screen eight years later in "Dr. No," his British pedigree was restored and the American CIA agent was once again named Leiter, *Felix* Leiter (portrayed by a pre-"Hawaii Five-O", Jack Lord).

Forty-nine years after Barry Nelson portrayed James Bond, we sat down to probe his recollections of the event. Joined by his wife Nansi, Barry Nelson admits to not realizing he had even played Bond until years later when it was pointed out to him.

"Casino Royale" limited edition litho signed by Barry Nelson and artist Jeff Marshall. Courtesy of Lee Pfeiffer, Spyguise

Barry Nelson in iconic Bond pose with gun, 2003. Photo © Richard E. Altman

No stranger to playing a Communist-chasing American agent, Nelson had portrayed Bart Adams on the first 26-episodes of CBS' 30-minute drama, "The Hunter." Working steadily since wrapping that program's first season, Nelson was playing the lead in a new CBS sitcom called "My Favorite Husband" (opposite actress Joan Caulfield) when the offer to play Bond in "Casino Royale" came.

Ironically, Nelson was on a much-needed vacation in Jamaica - the place where Fleming wrote his Bond adventures – and declined the offer. The rigors of live television had exhausted him and he had no desire to hurry back to the United States to begin rehearsal on another project. Neither Bond nor Ian Fleming were well known at the time, so there was no sense of literary or film history that caused him to reconsider.

It was only when he was told he would be playing opposite Peter Lorre that Nelson agreed to cut his vacation short and join the cast.

Peter Lorre pencil signature, circa 1938

Peter Lorre screen capture as Le Chiffre in "Casino Royale"

"I didn't read the original book," said Nelson. "I didn't have time."

Rehearsals for "Casino Royale" began immediately. The teleplay was co-written (with Anthony Ellis) by veteran screenwriter Charles Bennett whose credits include such Alfred Hitchcock classics as "The Man Who Knew Too Much" (1934), "The 39 Steps" (1935), "Secret Agent" (1936), "Sabotage"(1936), "Young and Innocent," (1937) and "Foreign Correspondent (1940).

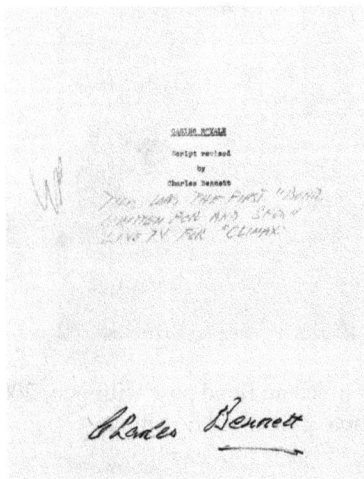

Original script for 1954 production of "Casino Royale" signed by renowned screenwriter and co-author Charles Bennett. *Courtesy of the Michael Van Blaricum Collection*

As for working with Lorre, Nelson recalls the experience was worth giving up the vacation for.

"Even in between acts we'd talk...it was fine...we enjoyed each other's company.

"Our longest scene," recalls Nelson, "was the one in the bathtub."

As the drama reaches its denouement, Lorre as arch villain LeChiffre has Bond placed in a bathtub and tortures him, forcing bound up Bond girl Valerie Mathis (played by Linda Christian), to watch in horror, but not allowed to scream.

Said Nelson: "*that* was not fun to act. To be the one that has to wince...how many different ways can you show pain...that's not fun to play."

As for his Bond girl Linda Christian, Nelson smiled. "I've known her since the MGM days. She was fine, except she had other things on her mind with that divorce thing."

"That divorce thing" was the unraveling of her marriage to Tyrone Power. The divorce would not become final until 1956.

Dubbed "*the anatomic bomb*" by the Hollywood publicity machine of the day, Linda Christian also has the distinction of appearing in Johnny Weissmuller's last star turn as the Lord of the Jungle in "Tarzan and the Mermaid" (1948). Among her other screen credits are "Slaves of Babylon" (1953); "Athena" (1954)"; The Devils Hand" (1961), and "The V.I.P.s with Richard Burton and Elizabeth Taylor (1963).

Linda Christian died of colon cancer in Palm Desert, California on July 22, 2011. She was 87 years old.

In addition to his distinction as the first portrayer of a Bond villain (and the reason that Barry Nelson became the screen's first James Bond), Peter Lorre is renowned for countless memorable film roles in landmark films across two continents and three decades. Peter Lorre died of a stroke on March 23, 1964. He was 59 years old.

Reflecting on his own career, Nelson considered himself first and foremost a stage actor and notably, a *working* actor whose career spanned decades on stage, in film and on television. His retirement years were filled largely with travels with wife Nansi and their mutual passion for antique collecting.

The couple maintained residences in Manhattan, Bucks County, Pennsylvania and a house in the French wine country that dates back to the 1400s, that Nelson said, *"we got a great deal on."*

As we concluded our session in September 2003 Nelson said simply, *"It's such a privilege to go places with my wife. We have wonderful conversations and laughter."*

Barry Nelson died April 7, 2007 while traveling with his wife in Bucks County, Pennsylvania. He was 89 years old.

CLIMAX! production of 'Casino Royale' featuring Peter Lorre as Le Chiffre,
Barry Nelson as James Bond and in background, Linda Christian as Valerie Mathis.
Image dated October 21, 1954. Photo courtesy of CBS Television.

A Bond for All Ages...

My Dad took me to my first Bond movie. It was a "boy's night out" – just me and him – and I treasured those occasions. That first exposure to Bond was actually the series' second big screen adventure, "From Russia With Love." It was 1964, I was 11 and most people I knew were still pronouncing the lead actor's name "*Seen.*" When pointed to the correct pronunciation of "Shawn" I wondered how the heck they got an H sound out of S-e-a-n.

But baby I was hooked on Bond, and like an evangelical, I began hooking my friends, cousins and anyone who would listen to my detailed recaps. I acted out the fight on the Orient Express with a school friend; retold the stories, and spoke knowingly of things like skin suffocation suffered by exotic dancers covered in paint (*you need to keep one patch of skin at the base of the spine clear to let the skin breathe*) and the advantages of a Walther PPK versus a Beretta (*doesn't jam, has a delivery like a brick through a plate glass window and can be fit with a silencer with negligible reduction in velocity*). If only I could smoke cigarettes from a cigarette case (*OK...one negative influence*), drink champagne and martinis (shaken, not stirred) and wear a tuxedo, the world would be mine. Figuring out that whole woman thing would take longer.

Ahh,..the lessons of my pre-teen youth.

It was a little while before I got to see the series' first installment, "Dr. No", but thanks to United Artists' liberal (and profitable) re-release policy with the Bond films, I did not have to wait years until it came to television. Home video was still in the Super 8 silent stage; there were no videocassettes or DVDs to pop into a player at will or whim. The upside was I got to watch these over-sized adventures over and over again, on a *really* big screen, in a darkened theater with an audience of like-minded acolytes. That ambience gave even greater scale to what was already a larger-than-life experience.

A series of circles travel across a blackened screen...Perhaps they are searchlights, the lenses of a binocular or a high-powered scope. Finally one stops and morphs into a gun barrel...the barrel's internal rifling frames the scene as James Bond enters. The camera pans with him. Now within the eye-like frame of that gun barrel, Bond stops, turns and fires...and a curtain of blood rings down over the scene. The gun barrel moves off, Bond and the blood fade out and that circular spotlight zooms in on the pre-title action sequence of virtually every James Bond movie of the last 50 years.

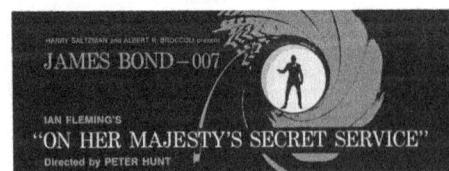

Detail of James Bond Opening Title Design, signed by its creator Maurice Binder. Courtesy of the Michael Van Blaricum Collection.

It is almost Pavlovian for Bond fans. Sitting there in the darkened movie house with *Twizzlers* or *Goobers* or the time-honored bucket of pop corn, watching those circles appear on the screen, the opening strains of the James Bond theme are introduced at full crescendo, followed by what was once described as a "twangy electric guitar" vamp as Bond strolls on to the screen. It is as iconic a moment as the first, "Bond, James Bond," as clichéd as the first "shaken not stirred," and as inevitable as the high-stakes, high-energy action to follow.

Like Joseph Caroff and the 007 logo, the man who designed James Bond's opening title sequence did so for "Dr. No," and did it a half-century ago. Renowned as one of the great title designers in movie history, Maurice Binder's work can be seen on 14 James Bond films and countless other motion pictures. And though it too has been modified over the years, Binder's original design concept is manifest and continues to this day. Like so many other elements in the series, it is quintessentially *"Bondian."*

On November 3, 2011 – 50 years to the day that Producers Harry Saltzman and Albert R. "Cubby" Broccoli announced that an actor named Sean Connery would be portraying 007 in the first big screen Bond adventure -- principal photography began in London on official Bond film number 23. Entitled "SkyFall," it continues traditions set by previous Bond pictures including exotic location shoots. In this latest case, the action follows Bond to China, Turkey (for the first time since "From Russia With Love") and a castle in Scotland.

Eunice Gayson, formally attired as Silvia Trench in the casino scene in Dr.No as provided the opening for Bond's iconic introduction to film audiences and reprised her role in "From Russia With Love." Eunice Gayson's daughter Kate played in a casino scene in "Goldeneye."

Though Bond films typically make stars of their cast members, producers Barbara Broccoli and her half-brother Michael Wilson have tapped an already stellar cast and crew for "SkyFall." Academy Award Winning director Sam Mendes ("American Beauty") puts his stamp on the franchise, along with Academy Award winning actor Javier Bardem ("No Country for Old Men") as the latest Bond villain. Two-time Oscar nominee Ralph Fiennes and five-time Oscar nominee Albert Finney round out the top line cast which includes Dame Judi Dench returning as "M" and Daniel Craig returning for his third turn as 007. The two newest additions to the "Women of Bond" club are English Actress Naomie Harris (of "Pirates of the Caribbean" fame) as a field agent named Eve, and French actress Bérénice Marlohe playing (in her words), "a glamorous, enigmatic character named Séverine.

By this time next year – amidst a whirlwind of publicity and "Golden Anniversary" commemorations -- "SkyFall" will be in theaters. The number of Bond women (no longer Bond *girls*) varies depending on whether one counts both the villainous and virtuous ones. Suffice it to say, that exclusive club has expanded big time since Ursula Andress as "Honey Rider" stepped out of the surf wearing a white bikini with a dive knife slung low across her hip. The Andress standard (if not the exact look) for future Bond girls/women was set.

Just how iconic is Ursula Andress? When the bikini she was wearing in that scene was sold at a London Christie's auction of Bond memorabilia on Valentine's Day 2001, the image of Ursula wearing it was on the auction catalog cover. *The hammer came down when the final bid of $61,500 was reached.*

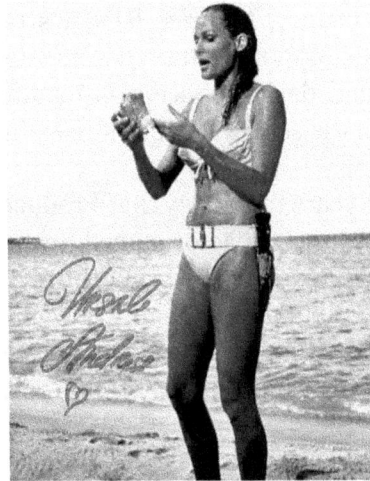

Bikini clad Ursula Andress as "Honeychile Rider" in "Dr. No" (1962)
Courtesy of the Alexander Brauchle Collection

Forty years after the release of "Dr. No," Bond producers paid homage to Ursula's inaugural appearance when Halle Berry stepped out of the surf in "Die Another Day," wearing an orange bikini with a dive knife slung across *her* hip. The cultural recall was instantaneous and worldwide. *As were the cheers.*

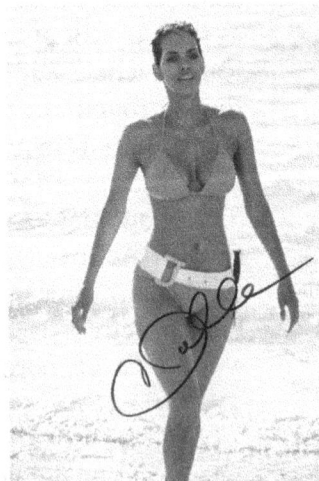

Bikini clad Halle Berry as "Jinx" in "Die Another Day" (2002)

The villain in "Dr. No" was played by Canadian born stage and screen actor Joseph Wiseman. Despite a brilliant and varied acting career, he was reportedly distressed that he is best remembered for his portrayal of the diabolical Dr. No. Nonetheless his contribution to the Bond film legacy remains intact as ever. Wiseman died in New York in October 2009 at the age of 91.

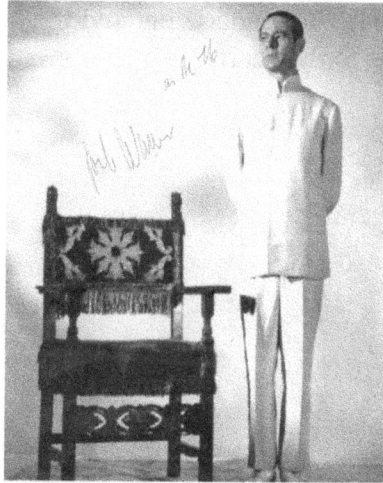

Joseph Wiseman as "Dr. No"

My first Bond girl was Italian actress Daniela Bianchi playing a Russian operative named Tatiana Romanova in "From Russia With Love." (It all made perfect sense in 1964). Still, Bond fans frequently cite her as among their favorite leading ladies, and in fact often cite "From Russia With Love" as their favorite or among their favorite Bond movies of all time.

Daniela Bianchi as Tatiana Romanova in promotional picture with
Sean Connery for "From Russia With Love"

The rarest of all "From Russia With Love" autographs belongs to veteran Mexican actor Pedro Armendariz, playing the role of Bond's Turkish ally Ali Kerim Bey. Though only 51 years old, Armendariz was dying of cancer when he took the role, seeing it as an opportunity for a last, substantial payday to leave as an inheritance for his family. Fittingly, it remains the most universally recognized performance of his career.

Out of regard for his condition, the Bond producers filmed all of his scenes at the beginning of the production and in rapid succession, ensuring that Armendariz could complete his portion of the filming. At the conclusion of his scenes (and well before production on the film wrapped), Armendariz entered the hospital and, on June 18, 1963 ended his own life with a bullet to the heart.

Signature of Pedro Armendariz on a card

Unsigned still of Pedro Armendariz as Kerim Bey in
"From Russia With Love"

There are no known signed images of Pedro Armendariz as Kerim Bey in "From Russia With Love" as the film's publicity photos had not yet been published when he died. As a result only non-Bond related signed images, paper autographs and cuts are available to collectors.

Footnote: The actor's son Pedro Armendariz, Jr. played the role of the corrupt President of the fictional Central American nation Isthmus, in the 16th Bond film, "License to Kill" (1989), opposite Timothy Dalton as Bond.

It is in "From Russia With Love" that we first meet Ernst Stavro Blofeld, head of the villainous organization *SPECTRE*. Well, we don't so much meet him as his hand, his measured, menacing voice and his trademark white cat. The camera would not reveal the face of Blofeld until the franchise's fifth installment, "You Only Live Twice."

The villains wo do meet in "From Russia With Love" are formidable. The ruthless ex-soviet intelligence agent Rosa Klebb was played with poisonous demeanor (and more than a little Lesbian subtext) by stage star Lotte Lenya. The lady of the poisonous stiletto-*tipped* shoes proved a worthy and resourceful enemy for Bond. Joining her in villainy was Robert Shaw as the sociopathic SPECTRE enforcer Donald "Red" Grant.

For collectors of Bond autographs, these are two of the most difficult to find, at least on Bond material. Though Lenya's signature can be found on images, Playbills and record albums from her long and illustrious stage career, signed Rosa Klebb material is scarcer and correspondingly pricey.

Robert Shaw's impressive array of film credits transcends his role in "From Russia With Love" (thus creating greater demand for his signature). Best known for his portrayal of the edgy and shark obsessed sea captain Quint in "Jaws" (1975), Shaw also turned in a brilliantly ruthless performance as mobster Doyle Lonnegan in "The Sting" (1972) opposite Paul Newman and Robert Redford. Sadly, Shaw died of a heart attack in 1978 at the age of 51, cutting short a life and a career that no doubt would have created far more iconic movie memories (and presumably more autographs for his fans).

If "Dr. No" and "From Russia With Love" laid the foundation for five decades of Bond films, it was the third installment in the franchise, "Goldfinger" that laid out the formula for virtually all future Bonds. Bond's popular tricked out attaché case in "From Russia With Love" led producers to develop Bond's tricked out Aston Martin DB5 in "Goldfinger."

Having more in common with a fighter jet than a sports car, the once and forever "James Bond car" had "front wing machine guns" behind the headlights, an ejector seat (passenger side only), smoke screen, bullet proof shield and some nasty, telescoping wheel hub 'knock off caps' that bring to mind the climactic chariot race in "Ben Hur".

German actor Gert Frobe as the titular villain "Goldfinger"

Then too there was Connery's Bond, fit for action and displaying a sardonic wit only hinted at in earlier pictures. The villainous object of Bond's attention was *"Auric Goldfinger"* (in cahoots with the 'Red' Chinese); Goldfinger's lethal and mute Korean manservant *"Odd Job"* and of course, the beautiful and resourceful villain turned good-girl, iconically named, *"Pussy Galore."*

In his pre Odd Job days, Harold Sakata worked as a professional wrestler under the name Tosh Togo. Periodically, souvenir fan card photos signed with that name come to market. Though more obscure, his Sakata signature – particularly on an Odd Job image – continues to be the most desirable.

Harold Sakata as Odd Job in "Goldfinger"

Harold Sakata signature with drawing of Odd Job's lethal steel rimmed bowler hat. Sakata's signature is among the most in-demand and rarest pieces in any Bond collection. Both images courtesy of the Alexander Brauchle Collection.

While Fleming often created imaginative and evocative names for his female characters (and Pussy Galore was definitely one of his creations), the movie franchise created new female characters with equally suggestive names. Witness "Diamonds Are Forever's" buxom *Plenty O'Toole* (*"named after your father perhaps"* quips Bond); *Dr. Holly Goodhead* ("Moonraker"), Olympic nymphet *Bibi Dahl* ("For Your Eyes Only"), *Xenia Onatopp* ("Goldeneye"). *Dr. Molly Warmflash* ("The World is Not Enough") *Miranda Frost* ("Die Another Day") and of course, the ever popular *Octopussy* from the film of the same name. (In the last instance, though the name Octopussy was a Fleming creation, it referred to an actual pet Octopus in the original short story and not a woman.).

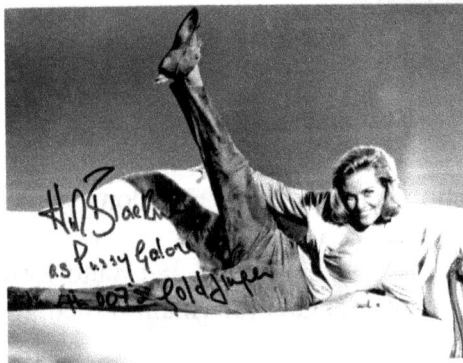

Honor Blackman as "Pussy Galore"

Maud Adams as "Octopussy"

Gallery: The Rarest of the Rare
(Including the impossible, the unusual and odd, and the one-offs)

Collectors call them "Holy Grail" pieces and they are often the driving force behind collectors not declaring their collection complete and moving on. A colleague once told me (only half-jokingly) that *"completionism"* – the drive to collect everything in a series – *"is a sickness."* Still, it is what drives many collectors and keeps them on their quests.

Herewith, a selection of "want list" wonders of the Bond world…

John Kitzmiller, 007's First Friend

John Kitzmiller played Bond's Cayman Islander ally Quarrel in "Dr.No" and was ultimately incinerated by the evil Dr.'s dragon tank. In real life, Kitzmiller died on February 23, 1965 at age 52, just three years after portraying Quarrel. While any John Kitzmiller signature is rare, signed Bond material is nearly unheard of and unseen. Indeed, the only two pieces I have ever heard of were sold recently by Alexander Brauchle's 007autographs. Alex graciously provided an exemplar of John Kitzmiller's signature for publication here.

John Kitzmiller's signature
Courtesy of the Alexander Brauchle collection.

John Kitzmiller as Quarrel in "Dr. No."

Bambi and Thumper… and Bambi?

Donna Garrat and Lola Larson have been the subject of questions and searches since their names were linked during the production of "Diamonds Are Forever." In a memorable scene, two athletic women named Bambi and Thumper take turns knocking Sean Connery's Bond from pillar to post before Bond prevails (of course!) employing a proper swimming pool dunking to make them talk. Not exactly water boarding, but effective enough for the time.

According to Bond historian Tim Greaves, the original movie credits omitted crediting Thumper as actress Trina Parks (an oversight since corrected on countless VCR and

DVD copies of the movie). The actress who played Bambi was credited to a stuntwoman named Donna Garrat, who only appears briefly and then only on the Diamonds are Forever DVD's bonus documentary by John Cork. Apparently the actress who *actually* played Bambi was not an actress at all but a gymnast who was on the set to teach the actresses the tumbling moves. Depending on the reference resource, the part is credited to one or the other.

While Trina Parks does sign and makes occasional appearances at signing shows, locating either Donna Garrat or Lola Larson has been uniformly unsuccessful, making *both* of their autographs hotly sought after by collectors.

Two Girls, One Signature: Trina Parks signs as 'Thumper' in "Diamonds Are Forever" while Lola Larson's autograph as 'Bambi' is missing in action.

"Perhaps," writes Tim Greaves in his book, "The Bond Women 007 Style," a future Bond scholar will take up the reins and succeed in locating Miss Larson for her own recollections."

Sean Connery Lip Print and Autograph

For a guy with a reputation for not signing much, this fanciful piece is indeed a rarity.

Connery provided the lip print (with facial hair embellishment) along with his inscription and signature for a charity event conducted by the *Save the Children Fund* back in 1988. The "lipographs" were then sold at auction to raise money for the charity.

Sean Connery Lip Print and Autograph
Courtesy of the Alexander Brauchle
collection.

Double Life of a Wife...

Noted Australian actress Diane Cilento (L) – then married to Sean Connery (here without his Bond hairpiece) – is outfitted to double actress Mie Hama (R) in a swimming scene for "You Only Live Twice." Cilento and Connery had one son, Jason before divorcing in 1973. Diane Cilento died October 6, 2011, one day after her 78th birthday.

Tetsuro Tamba

Considered one of Japan's greatest actors, Tetsuro Tamba played Tiger Tanaka, chief of the Japanese Secret Service and an ally of Bond's in "You Only Live Twice" (1967). Tamba also served as a leader and spokesperson for a Japanese spiritual movement. Tamba died of pneumonia in 2006 at the age of 84.

Tetsuro Tamba as Tiger Tanaka in "You Only Live Twice" (1967)

The Scene…and the Poster Artist's Conception of the Scene.

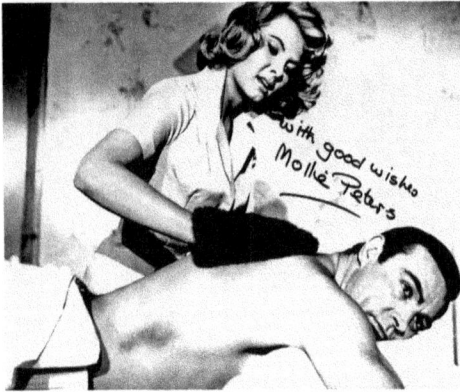

Mollie Peters as therapist Patricia Fearing in "Thunderball" gives Connery's Bond a sensual rubdown with a mink glove.

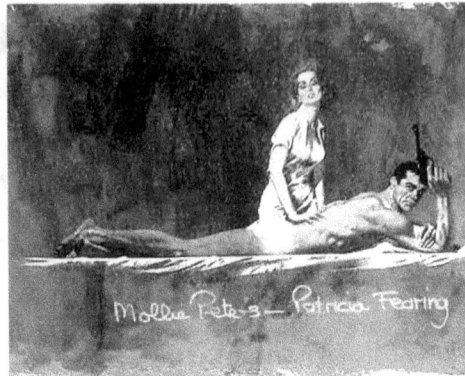

Artist's rendition of the scene deemed too hot for poster art. Similar artwork was used in some markets with Connery's bare bottom covered by swim trunks.

Fleming Books Signed by their Movie's Stars

Since Ian Fleming died nearly 47 years ago (and did not sign very many books), signed editions of his works are rare, and have become exceedingly expensive. To help fill that void, a popular trend in recent years has been to have the original Fleming novels signed by the stars of their corresponding films. The following examples are provided courtesy of the Brad Frank collection. Mr. Frank obtained all of the signatures personally, so their authenticity is without question.

"Thunderball" -- signed on the front free endpaper by Paul Stassino ("Francois Derval"); Luciana Paluzzi ("Fiona Volpe"); Mollie Peters ("Nurse Patricia Fearing"); and Martine Beswick ("Paula Caplan").
Footnote: Beswick also played one of the fighting Gypsy girls in "From Russia With Love."

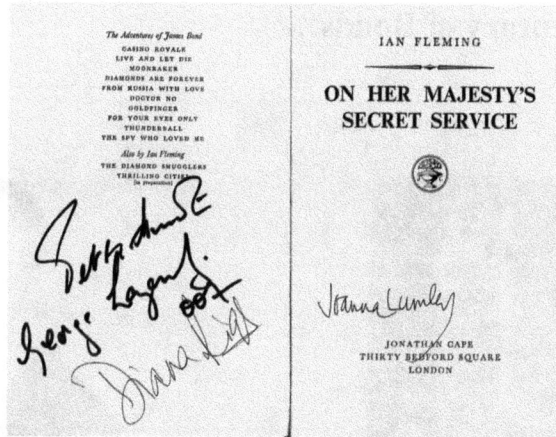

"On Her Majesty's Secret Service" -- signed by director Peter Hunt; George Lazenby ("James Bond"); Diana Rigg ("Tracy Di Vicenzo"); and Joanna Lumley ("English girl").

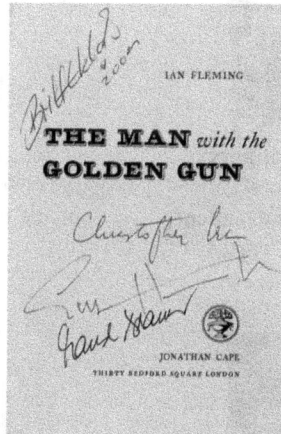

"The Man With The Golden Gun" signed by Britt Ekland ("Mary Goodnight"), Christopher Lee ("Francisco Scaramanga"); director Guy Hamilton; and Maud Adams ("Andrea Anders").
Footnote: Maud Adams returned to the Bond series as "Octopussy" in the film of the same name.

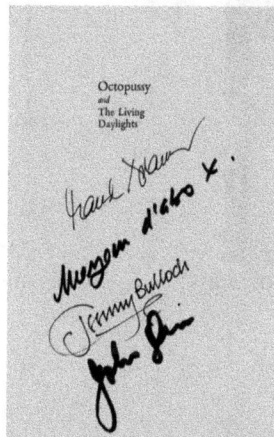

"Octopussy and The Living Daylights" -- signed by Maud Adams ("Octopussy"); Maryam D'Abo ("Kara Milovy"); Jeremy Bulloch (Q's assistant "Smithers"); and director John Glen.)

Gallery: A Half-Century of Bonds...

Sean Connery

Sean Connery as James Bond in "Goldfinger" (1964). Signed at the Caledonian Hotel in Edinburgh, Scotland 2010 (making it an excellent example of his *more recent* signature). Courtesy of the Alexander Brauchle Collection.

Sean Connery as James Bond in "Never Say Never Again" (1983), the only franchise Bond actor to go outside the franchise to play the role as well.

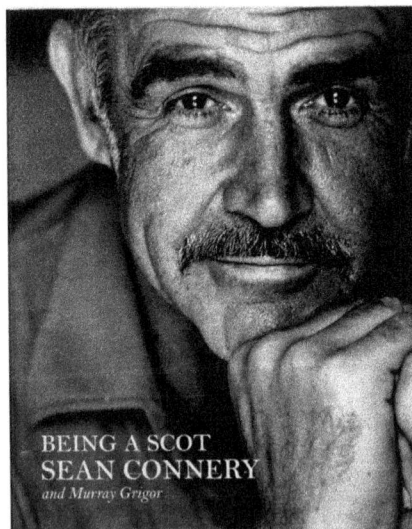

Cover of Sean Connery's quasi-autobiography "Being A Scot," (2008)

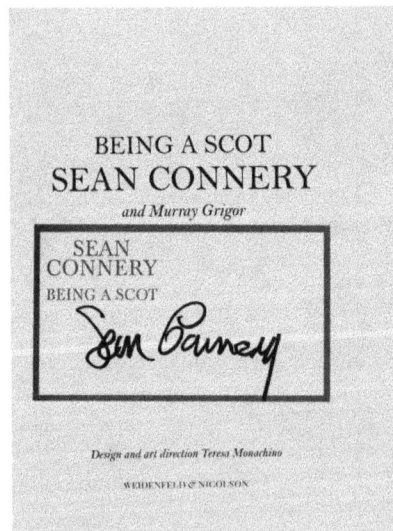

Boldly signed title page of Sean Connery's book "Being A Scot," (2008)

George Lazenby

George Lazenby as James Bond in "On Her Majesty's Secret Service" (1967)

George Lazenby poster art as James Bond in "On Her Majesty's Secret Service" (1967)

Roger Moore

Roger Moore strikes an iconic James Bond stance in "The Man With the Golden Gun" (1974)

Roger Moore swaps his tux for a spacesuit and Walther PPK for a Raygun and still manages to pull off a classic Bond pose in "Moonraker" (1979)

Roger Moore signing his autobiography "My Word is My Bond", NYC, November, 2008

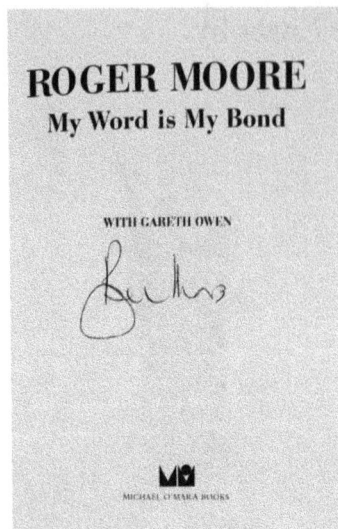

Title page of "My Word is My Bond" signed by Roger Moore, NYC, November 2008

Timothy Dalton

A *reversed* promotional photo of Timothy Dalton as James Bond from "The Living Daylights" (1987). Note the left-hand gripping gun and the right side part in his hair.

Timothy Dalton picks up the Walther PPK as James Bond in "License to Kill" (1989)

Pierce Brosnan

Pierce Brosnan as James Bond in a classic "gun up" promo pose – "Goldeneye" (1995)

Pierce Brosnan as James Bond with the Aston Martin "Vanish" (2002)

Pierce Brosnan as James Bond – "spit take"

Daniel Craig

Daniel Craig as James Bond in the poster art for "Casino Royale" (2006). Note the nearly complete signature.

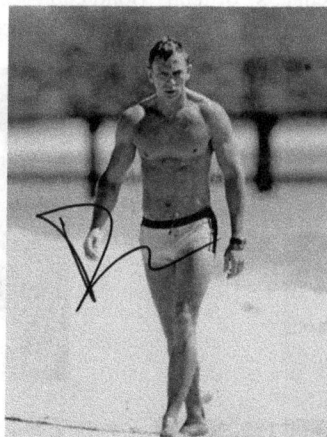

"*Bondcake*": Daniel Craig as James Bond in a swim trunks emerging from the surf in "Casino Royale" (2006). Note Craig's more typical "DC" signature.

Gallery: Portrayal Pairings

M & Ms:

Bernard Lee signature

Bernard Lee – Bond's original boss, through the first 11 Bond pictures, beginning with "Dr. No" (1962) and ending with "Moonraker" (1979)

Edward Fox - Bond's boss in the rogue "Thunderball" remake, "Never Say Never Again" (1983) that saw Sean Connery reprise the role of Bond one last time. The film was released opposite the franchise's "official" Bond entry for 1983, "Octopussy," starring Roger Moore.

Though *Robert Brown* made his Bond debut as Admiral Hargreaves in "The Spy Who Loved Me" he would not become "M" until "Octopussy" (1983) He played the role three more times in "A View to a Kill" (1985), "The Living Daylights" (1987) and "License to Kill" (1989).

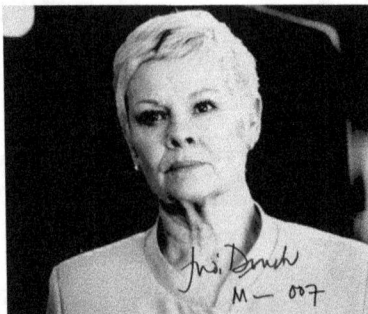

Dame Judi Dench took over the role of M in "Goldeneye" (1995) opposite the Bond debut of Pierce Brosnan and has made the part her own in every Bond picture since, including the most recent two starring Daniel Craig.   "SkyFall," the Bond film presently in production (also with Craig) will be her seventh appearance as "M."

Moneypenny's From Heaven:

Lois Maxwell – Played M's ever loyal and efficient secretary who had a bad case of the 'unrequiteds' for James Bond (whether he was played by Connery, Lazenby or Moore). She played the role through 14 films from "Dr. No" in 1962 to "A View To A Kill" in 1985.

Pamela Salem –Another cast member from the "unofficial" 1983 remake of "Thunderball," entitled "Never Say Never Again." Salem has the distinction of being the only actress to play Miss. Moneypenny opposite Sean Connery's Bond other than Lois Maxwell.

Caroline Bliss – Assumed the Moneypenny role when Timothy Dalton took over as James Bond in "The Living Daylights" (1987) and reprised it in "License To Kill" (1989)

Samantha Bond – Took over in 1995's "Goldeneye" and played the role of M's secretary opposite Pierce Brosnan in all four of his outings as Bond. Like her predecessors, she had a wicked crush on 007. Like Brosnan, her final appearance in Bond picture was "Die Another Day" in 2002.

"Q" & R & "Q" Again:

Where would Bond be without his gadget guru "Q" and where would "Q" be without the unflappable Desmond LLewelyn? Alas, that question got answered when Llewelyn died in 1999 at the age of 85. Llewellyn played "Q" in 17 Bond pictures beginning with "From Russia With Love" in 1963 to "The World Is Not Enough" in 1999. He was not in "Dr. No" (which featured the character 'Major Boothroyd' as the armorer). There was no role for "Q" scripted in "Live and Let Die" (Roger Moore's debut as Bond). LLewelyn returned as "Q" in the very next Roger Moore Bond outing, and remained in the role opposite Timothy Dalton and Pierce Brosnan.

Desmond LLewelyn composite photo as "Q"

Desmond Llewelyn signature

In 1999's "The World is Not Enough" producers included a reference to Q retiring soon, which would have made this Llewelyn's last Bond picture in any event. They also introduced Monty Python icon John Cleese as Q's rather clumsy assistant "R." By the time "Die Another Day" came around in 2002, Cleese's character, now less bumbling, had become the new "Q." Originally shorthand for "Quartermaster," the "Q" character has been eliminated from the grittier Bond films of the Daniel Craig era.

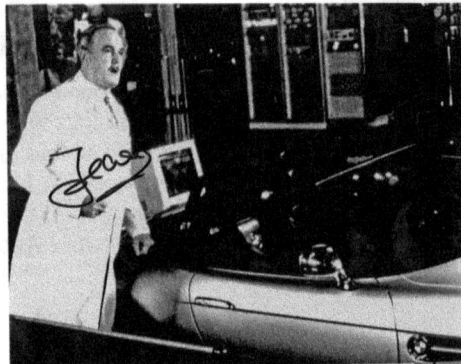

John Cleese as "R" in "The World Is Not Enough" with Bond's BMW Z 8

Largo e Molti Largo

Were it not for the presence of an alternate Emilio Largo (thanks again to "Never Say Never Again"), this signed Adolfo Celi image would have been filed in the rarities gallery. While Celi's signature is moderately hard to find, his scrawl on a Bond still or lobby card is more difficult to locate (and hence, more expensive). _As always, that also means, beware of forgeries._

The change of the character's first name – from Emilio in "Thunderball" to Maximiilian in "Never Say Never Again" – was likely due to the switch from the Italian actor Celi in the original to the Austrian actor Klaus Maria Brandauer in the remake.

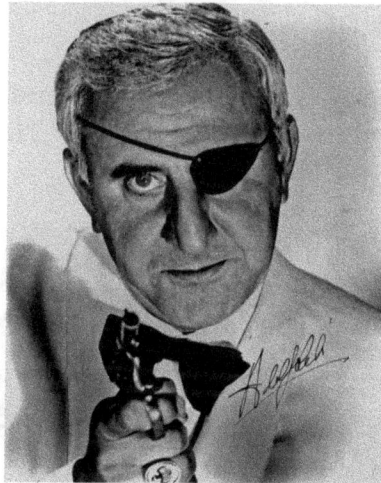

Adolfo Celi as the lead villain _Emilio_ Largo in "Thunderball" (1965)

Klaus Maria Brandauer as _Maximiilian_ Largo with Kim Basinger as Domino
(also signed) in "Never Say Never Again" (1983)

Playing Dominos

Gorgeous hot and French, Claudine Auger was producers Harry Saltzman and Cubby Broccoli's pick for the lead Bond girl in "Thunderball". Problem was, the character as written by Fleming (and in the original script) was Italian and named Domino Petachi. Apparently an Italian playing a Russian and a Mexican playing a Turk posed no problems for the producers in "From Russia With Love," yet for "Thunderball," Domino Petachi became the more French-sounding Domino Derval and brother Giuseppe Petachi became François Derval.

In the script, Domino's NATO pilot brother is killed (at Largo's direction) and replaced by a surgically altered doppelganger in order to steal a pair of nuclear warheads in a SPECTRE plot to blackmail the world.

When the remake "Never Say Never Again" was made, Kim Basinger was cast as Domino and the Petachi family name was restored. Her ill-fated pilot brother was renamed Jack Petachi.

Between Good and Evil: Claudine Auger as Domino Derval in "Thunderball"
surrounded by Sean Connery (L) and Adolfo Celi (R) (1965)

Two to Tango: Kim Basinger as Domino Petachi with Sean Connery
in "Never Say Never Again" (1983)

Five Faces of Blofeld

Though his face was obscured until the fifth Bond film, the head of SPECTRE's presence was felt in all but one of the first four films. No *identifiable* actor has played the role more than once. Anthony Dawson, who played the geologist (and Dr. No operative) Professor Dent before being summarily executed by Bond, went on to voice the role of Blofeld in "From Russia With Love" (1963) and "Thunderball" (1965).

Footnote: Charles Gray – Blofeld's incarnation in "Diamonds Are Forever" – previously portrayed Bond ally Dikko Henderson in "You Only Live Twice." Gray's character is dispatched with a dagger between the shoulder blades and dies in Bond's arms within minutes of their meeting.

Donald Pleasance as Ernst Stavro Blofeld in "You Only Live Twice" (1967)

Telly Savalas as Ernst Stavro Blofeld in "On Her Majesty's Secret Service" (1969)

Charles Gray as Ernst Stavro Blofeld in "Diamonds Are Forever" (1971)

John Hollis as Ernst Stavro Blofeld in "For Your Eyes Only" (1981)

Max Von Sydow as Ernst Stavro Blofeld in "Never Say Never Again" (1983)

Fighting Fakes and Forgeries

As any collector knows, spotting and avoiding fakes, forgeries (and even secretarials) particularly on rare or expensive pieces that you really *want* to be real, can be both a challenge and a gut check. Obviously, face-to-face encounters leave little chance for error, but knowing where a particular a subject will be when they will be there can be (and for some, is) a full-time job.

That leaves through the mail signings – balanced with seriously good exemplars or seriously knowledgeable experts to tell the difference between a secretarial (or autopen) from a truly hand-signed document or photo.

That leaves finding reliable dealers who do the heavy lifting for you, are not likely to get burned themselves. More importantly, if they *do* get burned, they value their reputation more than the cost of their own mistaken loss. Fortunately, in the world of James Bond there are dealers who can be relied upon for the authenticity of their product. This is not to say they are the only reliable ones…these are just the ones I know about and have dealt with.

The first is Alexander Brauchle, a German autograph dealer specializing in Bond material from signed pictures, documents, papers and cuts to props, costume pieces and promotional items. In business since 1997, Brauchle has been collecting Bond material for nearly 30 years. In addition to having an extensive selection of Bond material on his website – www.007autographs.com - he also provides exemplars of real and fraud signatures of the six film Bond actors, showing how their real autographs have changed over the years. The items for sale are searchable by film, by character type (i.e., villain, ally, small role player) and by the name of the actor. Finally, his COA is worth something for one reason: he stands behind what he sells. Brauchle is the source of many of the pieces used in this article, either because he provided the image for our use from his collection or I purchased the piece from him that is now in my collection.

Located in the UK, *Bondstars* utilizes in-person, private signings with Bond people from leading stars to behind the scenes specialists and creates special events for signing opportunities coinciding with the original release of a particular film to a tribute to some key figure. Occasionally, if they come across a classic autograph, they might offer it, but as founder Gareth Owens says, " they are one-off and few and far between…We deal primarily with in-person signed autographs, witnessed by us"

Bondstars was founded in 2002 at the suggestion of George Lazenby who was in the UK for the Bond 40th Anniversary press and promotional events and autograph signing shows. "At the end of his two weeks he had a little bundle of pics left over and said, "Hey if I sign and leave these with you and you can offload them, I'll cut you in on any deal."

Maud Adams, Lois Chiles and Eunice Gayson thought that was a fine idea and got on board as well. In short order, Bondstars set up a 'one-stop shop' website –

www.Bondstars.com – for the stars to sell their own photos and the company's sterling reputation among the stars and collectors grew.

"A year or so later, Richard Kiel (JAWS) was coming to London to promote his autobiography and asked if we could set anything up for him," Bondstars arranged 14 events over 16 days for him in and around London, including a stop at Cambridge University where Kiel delivered an address and an afternoon reception at Pinewood Studios (home of the "Bond Stage") that consisted of a fan Q&A session, autograph signings and a studio tour.

Since then says Owen "we have held a Pinewood gathering every year since and have welcomed guests from George Lazenby to Roger Moore, Honor Blackman, Britt Ekland, Maud Adams, Maryam D'abo and many others…"

Today, Bondstars represents more than 75 Bond cast members, crew and authors.

"Sir Christopher Lee, Britt Ekland and Honor Blackman have all stated they no longer sign through the mail due to the quantities of requests they began receiving," reveals Owen. "They have their own websites of course, and direct people there or to us. Sir Christopher told us that his secretary uses a stamp on unsolicited photographs mailed to him now. I'm sure it's a common practice by many.

"Sir Roger Moore occasionally signs for UNICEF, as does Sir Sean Connery for his Scottish charities. But they receive hundreds of requests, and there can only be so much time in a day. That's probably why autograph hunters have become so aggressive and rude – thinking the harder you push or shout, the better chance you'll have…

"In contrast, in New York, two guys waited outside Sir Roger's hotel and said "Excuse me sir, would you mind signing an autograph for us?" Roger said "sure". They reached in to their bag, produced one still, thanked him and happily walked off. *That* was a pleasant experience."

Lee Pfeiffer of *SpyGuise* is less an autograph dealer than he is a resource for vintage Bond Books, magazines and memorabilia. The founder and editor of *Cinema Retro* magazine and the co-author of a handful of books on the subject of Bond, Pfeiffer does offer some highly collectible, signed pieces and does so at reasonable prices (given the item).

Among Pfeiffer's cache of *signed* Bond related material are first edition, *hardcover* copies of the book "Q The Biography of Desmond Llewelyn," signed by LLewelyn shortly before his death in 1999. Pfeiffer also commissioned artist Jeff Marshall to create a series of limited edition lithographs that harked back to the traditions of the old Bond movie poster art. Done with the blessings of (and license from) EON Productions, the line of signed lithos was thought to be sold out. Recently, Pfeiffer came upon a few remaining pieces of the poster they created as a retrospective for the 1954 TV production of "Casino Royale," signed and numbered by both Jeff Marshall and the program's star,

Barry Nelson. Pfeiffer has also turned up a few pieces of "The Man With the Golden Gun" lithos, again signed and numbered by Marshall as well by the golden gun man himself, Christopher Lee.

Four of a kind...

Rittenhouse George Lazenby Autograph Card

Rittenhouse Roger Moore Autograph Card

Rittenhouse Pierce Brosnan Autograph Card

Rittenhouse Daniel Craig Autograph Card

Trading Card images courtesy of Rittenhouse Archives

Arguably, the most unorthodox way for a Bond autograph collector to acquire a desired signature is the trading card route. Still, it is becoming a reliable way to obtain legitimately signed, authentic (and licensed pieces) which establishes provenance for the piece in the years to come. The keeper of the Bond license for trading cards over the past decade or so is a company out of Philadelphia called Rittenhouse Archives. Rittenhouse may well be with the world's largest producer of *non-sport* trading cards.

The very randomness of the autograph card insertions (two autograph cards in every box of 24 packages of cards) means that there is no guarantee which signatures will be found in any given box.   As a result a secondary market of trading card dealers has developed. These dealers buy up cases of the cards and split the packs, culling autograph cards and other desirable inserts for individual sale at premium prices. The remaining cards are broken up into inexpensive common card sets and mini-master sets of varying descriptions that include less desirable premium insert cards.

These are then most often marketed to waiting fans on, (dare I say it)....*eBay*.

Fact is, acquiring autographs on eBay from a pack of Rittenhouse Bond cards (or from the autograph dealers mentioned in this article) may well be the most reliable way of buying an autograph on that auction site and *not* getting burned. Still, the individual card dealers will often place exorbitant prices on some of the most desirable cards. Indeed they may often be getting more for trading card than the same image would fetch as a signed 8x10 glossy.

Steven Charendoff, founder and President of Rittenhouse points out that part of the reason for the secondary market prices is the "perception and reality of scarcity combined with the consumer's knowledge that our process is legitimate, the numbers of sets we produce is limited and are distributed worldwide, not just in the United States. They have a comfort level with us."

That comfort level comes at a price for Charendoff as well. The stars are paid for their signatures and verification of authenticity is done with photographs and video of the signing(s) as well as a signed and witnessed affidavit from the signing stars. While those still and video images are on file at Rittenhouse, part of the agreement with the stars is that they *not* be used for publicity purposes as the signings are often done at home during private and very casual times.

Charendoff recounts a Bond card signing with Barbara Bach that yielded an unexpected bonus. Bach played the Soviet agent Anya Amasova opposite Roger Moore's Bond in "The Spy Who Loved Me."

"Barbara Bach signed the cards for us back in 2003/04. At the end, she signed the release document attesting to the fact that she had signed the cards. The release also required that a witness sign and Barbara Bach's husband, Ringo Starr was the witness. It was the first time the witness signature was worth more than the star's."

Of the thousands of Bond cards produced over the years, there have been two notable holdouts: Sean Connery and Timothy Dalton. Charendoff points out that, "it took us about ten years to get Pierce Brosnan...sometimes you just haven't found the right person to make the recommendation to the star and to assure them that everything is on the up and up."

Rittenhouse's license to sell James Bond trading cards continues with EON and one can expect a new set of Bond cards when the latest Bond adventure opens in 2012.

All autographs used in this article are from the Richard E. Altman collection except where credited otherwise.

Thanks to:
Mike Van Blaricum
Brad Frank
John Cork/Made in Cloverland
Tim Greaves
Alexander Brauchle
Lee Pfeiffer/Spyguise
Gareth Owen/Bondstars
Steve Charendoff/Rittenhouse Archives
Joseph Caroff
The late Barry Nelson and,
to Ian Fleming, Cubby and Harry, Barbara and Michael without whom…

Prisoner of War Covers From Jefferson Davis

By Brian M. Green

While prisoner of war covers from both sides during the War Between the States have been rather thoroughly discussed, little of anything has been written about correspondence from the high Confederate officials incarcerated after the collapse of the Confederacy. Among these officials was the former executive, President Jefferson Davis.

Upon the evacuation of Richmond on April 2, 1865, President Davis left by train and arrived in Danville, Virginia the next morning. When the news of General Lee's surrender at Appomattox (April 9) reached Davis, he then moved on to Greensboro, North Carolina for a conference with Generals Beauregard and Johnston. After deciding that General Johnston should attempt negotiations with General Sherman, President Davis proceeded with his Cabinet and staff toward Charlotte, North Carolina. Upon his arrival there on April 18, he learned of the assassination of Abraham Lincoln. This sad event affected the armistice between Generals Johnston and Sherman which then expired on April 26. After its expiration, Davis, accompanied by some members of his Cabinet, his personal staff, and a detachment of cavalry, rode out of Charlotte with the object of reaching the Trans-Mississippi Department from which he hoped to either continue the war or effect a more favorable peace treaty.

On May 10, while in camp near Irwinville, Georgia, Davis and those accompanying him were captured by a Union detachment of the 4th Michigan Cavalry under the command of Col. Benjamin D. Pritchard. Among those captured with Davis were Vice President Alexander H. Stephens, Postmaster General John H. Reagan, Maj. Gen. Joseph Wheeler, Govenor Lubbock of Texas, Clement C. Clay, and Burton Harrison, private secretary to Davis.

Proceeding via Macon, Atlanta, Savannah (via steamboat), and Hilton Head, the prisoners were transferred to the steamer *William P. Clyde* which cast anchor on May 19 at Hampton's Roads, Virginia instead of Washington, D.C. There, the prisoners were dispersed to various places (the family of Davis was returned to Savannah) with the exception of Clement Clay and Jefferson Davis, who were imprisoned in separate cells at Fortress Monroe.

During his confinement there (May 22, 1865 to May 13, 1867), the correspondence of Davis was severely restricted. An extract from the OFFICIAL RECORDS, Volume 8, Series 3 on the handling of the ex-president's mail reads as follows:

WAR DEPARTMENT, ADJUTANT-GENERAL'S OFFICE,
August 18, 1865
Maj. Gen. N. A. Miles, U.S. Volunteers,
Commanding, &c., Fort Monroe, VA.:

SIR: Your letters of the 15th and 16th instant have been submitted to the Secretary of War.

Any letters which Mr. Davis desires to send his wife must relate only to family matters and be first submitted to the Attorney General's inspection. I return the letters from Mrs. Clay. The Secretary authorizes you to deliver the one addressed to her husband.

I am, sir, very respectfully, you obedient servant,

E.D. TOWNSEND,
Assistant Adjutant-General.

Two covers showing such usage are illustrated below. The first went to Washington, D.C. where it was censored by Attorney General James Speed (upper right corner) and then postmarked Nov. 25, 1865. When the letter arrived in Augusta it was not immediately delivered to Mrs. Varina Davis, who apparently was not in that city at that time. It was advertised and handstamped such on December 5, in addition to be struck with a straighline "UNCLAIMED." The second cover is also censored by Attorney General Speed and postmarked in Washington, D.C. on December 9, 1865.

According to Dr. Craven's accounts in his book The Prison Life of Jefferson Davis, (Carleton, New York, 1866)

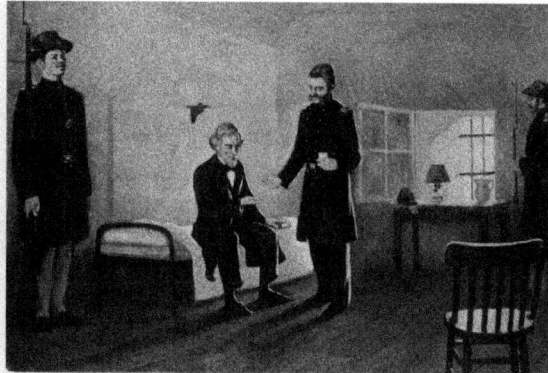

Jefferson Davis and Dr. Craven at Fort Monroe, Virginia

The prisoner complained bitterly of the restriction inposed by General Miles on his correspondence with his wife; certain subjects, and those perhaps of most interest, being forbidden to both. The convicts in State prisons were allowed this liberty unimpeded, or only subject to the supervision of the Chaplain, whose scrutiny had a religious and kindly character – that of a Father Confessor. His letters, on the contrary, had to be sent open to General Miles, and from him, he understood, open to the Attorney General. What unbosoming of confidence – mutual griefs, mutual hopes, the interchange of tender sympathies – was possible, or would be delicate under such a system! He pictured idle young staff officers, or yet more pitiful clerks in the Law Department at Washington, grinning over any confessions of pain, or terms of endearment, he might be tempted to use; and this thought embittered the pleasure of such correspondence might otherwise have conferred. The relationship of husband and wife was the inner vestibule of the temple – the holy of holies – in poor human life; and who could expose its secrets, or lay his heart bare on his sleeve, for such daws to peck at? Even criminals condemned to death for heinous crimes were allowed not only free correspondence with their wives, but interviews at which no jailor stood with earshot. What possible public danger could there be from allowing such letters to pass without scrutiny? Time will set all these petty tyrannies in their true light... If the privilege were ever abused – if anything he wrote to his wife were published to the detriment of the government, or tending to disturb the peace, what easier to say, "This privilege has been abused, and must cease?"

This kind Union Army doctor from Newark, New Jersey gradually succeeded in relieving the harsh conditions from the casement confinement and, after four and one-half months, was able to get Davis moved to a better place in the fort.

Today, one may visit Fortress Monroe and see exhibits pertaining to the role of the fortress during the war as well as the casemate in which Davis was confined. It is well worth the trip.

Bettie Page – A Pin-Up Icon

By Todd Mueller

Back in the early 1990's I saw an outfit named Glamourcon selling some books signed by Bettie Page. I had never heard of her but they were selling for a lot of money and the model looked like the girl next door. I contacted the owner of the company and he was vague only telling me that Bunny Yeager had discovered her back in the 1950's, that Bettie was reclusive and nobody knew exactly where she lived or if she was alive at all.

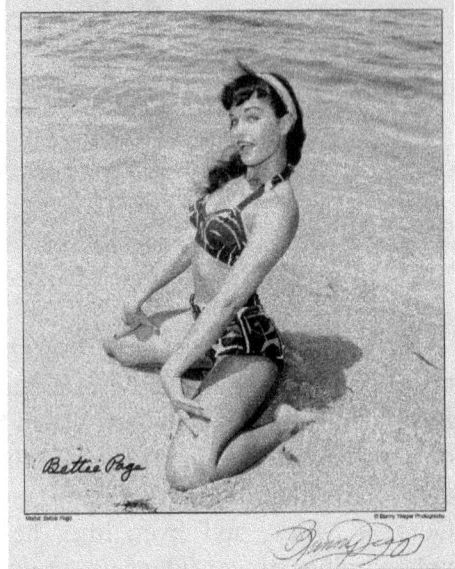

Enjoying the hunt for interesting things I started to call around. One person thought she had passed away comparing her to Elvis sighting's another told me she lived in Turkey not wanting to be bothered so finally I contacted Bunny Yeager the photographer. Bunny told me that years ago she and Bettie had a falling out because Bunny was making money of the photographs and Bettie felt she should be paid as well. Bettie didn't understand that Bunny photographed many models in the early 1950's, most all of which never amounted to anything. When Bunny would do this she would have the model sign a contract giving Bunny the exclusive rights to the images she took. Bunny would then try to sell the different photographs to magazines and Bettie always sold but Bettie was paid as a model for the day and wasn't entitled to future revenues earned at a later time. That's how their agreement's took shape back in the early 1950's and why they had a falling out some 40 years later.

I asked Bunny if she felt Bettie would entertain doing a signing and Bunny told me that would absolutely be out of the question but that I should contact Jack Page, Bettie's older brother out of Nashville, TN. So I did.

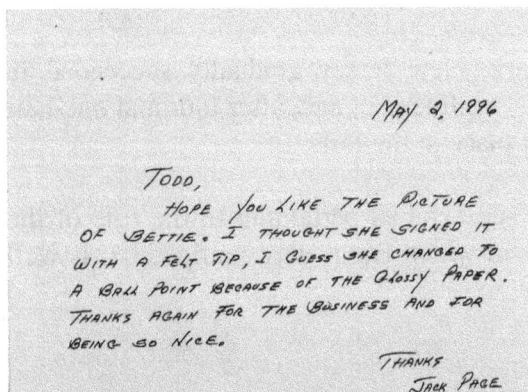

May 2, 1996

Todo,
Hope you like the picture of Bettie. I thought she signed it with a felt tip, I guess she changed to a ball point because of the glossy paper. Thanks again for the business and for being so nice.

Thanks
Jack Page

Jack was a great guy and what I didn't know at the time is that he won a purple heart in WWII and was considered somewhat of a celebrity himself. Jack was very cordial and kind with his sweet mannerism's and told me Bettie was a born again Christian and would never consider signing photographs, especially if they were nudes or Bunny Yeager images. Knowing Irving Klaw was the only other photographer to really capture Bettie from this time frame and his photographs were mostly of bondage

I knew if I was ever going to get Bettie to agree to sign her photographs it had to be with Bunny's images. Jack told me he would call his sister and ask but that she probably wouldn't be interested.

A few day's later Jack contacted me back and stated Bettie was not interested. I told him to tell her I would pay her $50 each. This shocked Jack who said he would mention that to her. I got a call back immediately and Bettie was in so for the first time ever Bettie agreed to sign Bunny Yeager nude's for me and my company. This signing sold out quickly so we did another. Years later, now into the late 1990's I was starting to get contacted by Hollywood and other's interested in representing Bettie on some level. Everyone had the same problems I initially had, How to reach her. It became quickly overwhelming so I suggested Bettie have an agent and they went with Curtis Management. Bettie began outselling Marilyn Monroe according to several and was a hit with Hugh Hefner also doing a limited edition item with Bettie.

One day I received a phone call from Bettie. She was miserable and living in an assisted living facility with two other women. She wanted out but needed money to find her own place. She had previously written me a letter stating I was paying her to much so I jumped at the opportunity. The condition was she didn't want me to go through CMG where they would take 40% of the money considering our relationship protected under some grandfather clause and if I would set her up in a hotel for the day she wouldn't feel bad about signing the photographs for me again. This time she agreed to sign for $5 per photo if I would send her $20,000.00. I did. It was our largest signing and the second to last one we would ever do with Bettie.

Bettie's story is currently in progress in a soon to be released film called; "Bettie Page Reveals all" produced by academy award nominated film producer Mark Moiri who sent me a movie poster from the film signing it; "Todd, thanks for your help in the film, Mark," which I have hanging in my office.

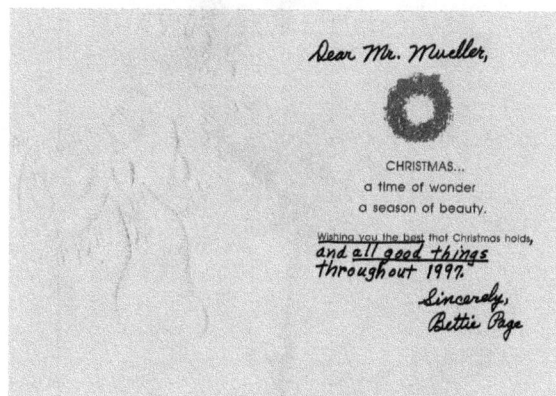

Bunny Yeager was once interviewed on a cable television show and she stated; "I (Bunny)was the one who discovered Bettie Page in the early 1950's, Todd Mueller rediscovered her in the 1990's."

Near the end of Bettie's life she was confined into the Patton State Mental hospital in California. Bettie had a long history of mental illness going in and out of mental institutions over the years. Her family asked me if I could become her power of attorney and attempt to get her out. It was futile because she had recently been diagnosed with chronic heart disease but I actually was looking into seeing if we could move Bettie Page into our home. Bunny Yeager, Jack Page and nieces and nephews all were on board if we could get her out of there but it wasn't meant to be.

The family asked if I would contact the Associated Press and announce her medical condition early in December of 2008 and I did stating Bettie was in a coma. This came as a shock to everyone and day's later, on December 11, 2008 I received a phone call from the associated Press telling me Bettie had passed away.

I was one of only a small handful of non-family members to be invited to Bettie's private funeral services in California where she was placed near Marilyn Monroe. Hugh Hefner, Mamie Van Doren, Dita Von Teese and others were present. Bettie was cremated and her niece honored my wishes to get me a lock of Bettie's hair. Bettie was one in a million. It's not very often to represent someone's signature for nearly 20 years. It's not often to talk to them, share stories about the holiday's, exchange Christmas cards, and have the family contact someone like me when their loved one, the celebrity needs help or assistance. Bettie was fun, wonderful and still beautiful until the end. She didn't like her photograph to be taken saying; "I want people to remember me the way I was." I have done hundreds of private signing's over the years but there was nobody like Bettie Page!

Leaders of the Soviet Union

By Dr. Zoltán Márián

Nikita Sergeyevich Krushchev / 1894-1971/
First Secretary of the Communist Party of the Soviet Union /1953-1964/
Chairman of the Council of Ministers of the Soviet Union / 1958-1964 /

Nikita Khrushchev was born in 1894 at Kalinovka near to the Ukraine border. He was the son of a mineworker. After the Russian Civil War Khrushchev became a miner. While working as a miner, he continued his education by attending high school. Khrushchev worked for the Communist Party in Kiev and then in Moscow. In 1935, he was appointed Secretary of the Moscow Regional Committee.

During World War II, he assisted military commanders fighting there, primarily in the Kursk Salient. In 1947, Stalin selected Khrushchev to reorganise the Soviet Union's agricultural production. After Stalin's death in 1953, he was appointed First Secretary of the Communist Party.

In January 1956, Khrushchev made his boldest move for power. At the XXth Party Congress he attacked Stalin and the 'cult of personality' he had developed. The 1956 Suez Crisis diverted the West's attention away from the USSR for a short time while the USSR's grip on the Warsaw Pact was increased when Hungary was invaded and the short-lived uprising brutally suppressed.

On March 27th 1958, Khrushchev also became Prime Minister of the USSR. Khrushchev gave the appearance of wanting to introduce a thaw in the Cold War and his appointment was greeted with cautious optimism in the West, especially after the austere rule of Stalin. However, his seeming feelers for peace were mixed with more hostile statements and Khrushchev became a hard man to predict – whether it was taking off his shoe and banging it on a table as he did at the United Nations.

By 1962 Khrushchev was worried that the Soviet Union was falling behind in the arms race. To restore the balance he conceived of a plan to place nuclear missiles on Cuba. His military advisors had assured him that the installation work could be done secretly. However on October 22nd, American reconnaissance aircraft discovered the missiles and the world was thrown into crisis. Khrushchev at first thought US President Kennedy would give in and he adopted a hard line. As the days went on, however, it became clear that the Americans were determined and would invade Cuba to remove the missiles. He had not intended to start a war over the matter and in fact many now say he won the contest. In return for the removal of Soviet missiles from Cuba he got the Americans to agree to remove theirs from Italy and Turkey and give a public promise not to invade Cuba.

The Cuban Missile Crisis was the first and only nuclear confrontation between the United States and the Soviet Union. The event appeared to frighten both sides and it marked a change in the development of the Cold War.

Leonid Brezhnev and other members of the Politburo dismissed Khrushchev on October 14, 1964, after Khrushchev's vacation at the Communist Party owned Black Sea resort. He was stripped of all privileges and lived under house arrest outside Moscow. After his death on September 11, 1971, Khrushchev was not buried officially like other Politburo members near the Kremlin. Instead, he was buried without an official ceremony at the Novodevichy Cemetery. The Cold War continued.

Krushchev travelled a lot. He met President Eisenhower, President Kennedy, de Gaulle, Adenauer, Indira Gandhi and the communist countries leaders of course. He visited Hungary four times. In his last visit he spent several days in Budapest in March-April 1964. He was popular in Hungary, he was interested in everything, he smiled always and he was very friendly. He and his wife Nina Petrovna did not like protocol they were much more different than other Soviet leaders. Hungarian town Bábolna was famous for horses. They presented a coach-and five horses show for Krushchev. He enjoyed the show very much. At the end, the leaders of the town gave the five horses with the coach to Krushchev – as a gift. He was very surprised but very happy.

Going back to Moscow – he travelled by train – his train stopped at the city of Debrecen railway station. Many thousand people were waiting for him including the delegation of Debrecen Pioneer Movement. Young teenagers belonged to this movement and they were lucky to talk to Krushchev for a minute. The delegation gave a small gift to the Soviet leader, who kindly signed the pioneer movement card – by red ball point pen. A photo was taken of Krushchev while he was standing on the train's step and this picture was fitted to the card next to the signature.

Leonid Ilyich Brezhnev /1906-1982/
Secretary-General of the Communist Party of the Soviet Union /1964-1982/
Chairman of the Presidium of the Supreme Soviet of the Soviet Union /1977-1982/

Brezhnev was born in 1906 in Dneprodzerzhinsk in the Ukraine. He studied engineering at his birthplace and worked in a metallurgical factory. He joined the Komsomol (Communist Youth Organization) in 1923. In 1931 Brezhnev became member of the Communist Party and he worked under Nikita Khrushchev. During the Second World War he served as a political commissar.

In 1952 Stalin invited him to join the Politburo. In 1964 Khrushchev was ousted and by the early 1970s Brezhnev had emerged as the most important political figure in the Soviet Union. His term in office was hallmarked by Soviet invasion of Czechoslovakia (1968) and Afghanistan (1977), domestic economic stagnation and persecution of dissidents. Brezhnev's health worsened in the winter of 1981–82. He rarely appeared in public during the spring, summer and the autumn of 1982. The official explanation by the Soviet government was that Brezhnev was not seriously ill, while at the same time doctors were surrounding him. He suffered a severel stroke in May 1982, but refused to relinquish office. Brezhnev died on November 10, 1982 after suffering a heart attack.

Brezhnev was "the great friend" of the communist Hungary, and a good friend of János Kádár, /1912-1989/ the First Secretary of the Hungarian Socialist Worker Party (Communist Party) as well.

I was a 15 year old student when I first wanted to have a Brezhnev signature. In the grammar school my Russian language teacher translated my letters into Russian language, but I never got any answer from Moscow. Soviet leaders did not respond private letters, and I understood that I would never receive his autograph this way.

In 1972 Brezhnev paid an official visit to Budapest. In a newspaper I saw a black and white photo showing both Brezhnev and Kádár. I wrote a letter to the Hungarian News Agency asking them, to send me a good quality photograph of the two leaders. The Agency sent me a big size photo.

I sent the photo to Kádár asking him to sign it, and I also asked him to forward the picture to "Comrade Brezhnev" for his autograph also. Some days later I received a letter from Kádár's Office telling me, that "Comrade Kádár has already signed the photo, and now we are going to comply with the second part of your request. It needs some time, so we ask your kind patience". About two months later, I received my photo back with both Kádár's and Brezhnev's signatures.

Twenty years later, I had the chance to talk with the Secretary of János Kádár. This person remembered that photo and told me, that the delegation had taken the photo to Moscow when Kádár visited Brezhnev on the following occasion, and Kádár personally asked Brezhnev to sign the photograph…

Alexei Nikolayevich Kosygin /1904-1980/
Chairman of the Council of Ministers of the Soviet Union / 1964-1980/

Kosygin was born in 1904 in St. Petersburg. Between 1938 and 1939 he served the city as mayor. In 1939, Kosygin became a member of the Central Committee of the Communist Party when he was appointed Commissar for the Textile Industry.

After World War II, Kosygin made his way up the party. Between 1948 and 1953 he was Minister of Finance and Minister of Light Industry as well as being a member of the Politburo. In 1957, he was given responsibility for economic planning and in 1960 was appointed Chairman of the State Economic Planning Commission and First Deputy Prime Minister.

After the Cuban Missile Crisis Kosygin took over Khrushchev's position as Chairman of the Council of Ministers. This effectively made him the USSR's Prime Minister.

As Prime Minister, he wanted to decentralise the control exerted by Moscow in industry and agriculture. Kosygin also wanted to provide the people of the USSR with more consumer goods. In this he was unsuccessful as the country was spending vast sums of money trying to keep up with the USA in military expenditure.

Kosygin resigned on October 23, 1980 as a result of poor health. He died eight weeks later. His death was not announced for three days, as Kosygin died on the eve of Brezhnev's birthday. He was buried in Red Square, Moscow.

His autograph is rare. Similar to Brezhnev, he did not answer for my letters either. Finally I met the Soviet Ambassador in Budapest, Hungary, who forwarded my letter and photo to the Prime Minister. Kosygin signed and dated the photo and it was returned to me via the Ambassador.

Nikolai Viktorovich Podgorny / 1903-1983 / Chairman of the Presidium of Supreme Soviet of the Soviet Union / 1965-1977/

Podgorny was born in the city of Karlovka in 1903. An engineer trained at the Technological Institute of the Food Industry in Kiev, he became deputy commissar of the Ukrainian food industry. In 1956 he was elected a member of the central committee of the party and of the presidium in 1960. In 1965 he became Head of State. He traveled widely and enhanced the position of president of the USSR. His meetings with Pope Paul VI in 1967 helped bring about more openness for the Catholic Church in Eastern Europe. He was relieved of his chairmanship and removed from the politburo in a 1977 power struggle with Brezhnev, who wished to combine the posts of Presidium Chairman and Party Secretary-General.

Podgorny died of cancer on January 12, 1983, and was buried in Moscow at the Novodevichy cemetery. In 1974 I got a signed card with a photo from him.

Andrei Andreyevich Gromyko / 1909-1989/ Chairman of the Presidium of Supreme Soviet of the Soviet Union /1985-1988/ Minister of Foreign Affairs / 1957-1985/

Gromyko, the son of peasants, was born near Minsk in Russia in 1909. After studying agriculture and economics he became a research scientist at the Soviet Academy of Science. He later joined the diplomatic service and went to Washington during the Second World War.

In 1943 Gromyko was appointed as the Soviet ambassador in the United States. In this post he attended the conferences in Teheran, Yalta and Potsdam. After the war he was made the Soviet permanent delegate to the United Nations. He also served as ambassador to Britain. Gromyko became Foreign Minister in 1957. He held the post for 28 years and during this period was the main Soviet negotiator with the United States government.

In 1985 Gorbachev relieved Gromyko of his duty as foreign minister and replaced him with Eduard Shevardnadze and Gromyko was appointed to the largely honorary position of Chairman of the Presidium of the Supreme Soviet. In 1988 Gromyko decided to leave Soviet politics for good. Gromyko recounts in his *Memoirs* that he told Gorbachev that he wished to resign before he made it official. The following day, October 1 1988, Gromyko sat beside Gorbachev, Yegor Ligachev and Nikolai Ryzhkov in the Supreme Soviet to make his resignation official.

During his twenty-eight years as Minister of Foreign Affairs Gromyko became the "number-one" on international diplomacy at home, renowned by his peers to be consumed by his work. Henry Kissinger once said "If you can face Gromyko for one hour and survive, then you can begin to call yourself a diplomat". An article written in 1981 in *The Times* said, "He is one of the most active and efficient members of the Soviet leadership. A man with an excellent memory, a keen intellect and extraordinary endurance. Maybe Andrey is the most informed Minister for Foreign affairs in the world". He met 9 American Presidents from FDR to Ronald Reagan. I am happy to have his signed photo he sent me as a Foreign Minister.

Yuri Vladimirovich Andropov / 1914-1984/
Secretary-General of the Communist Party of the Soviet Union / 1982-1984/

Andropov was the son of a railway official. He was educated at the Rybinsk Water Transport Technical College. He became a member of the Communist Party in 1939 and was First Secretary of the Central Committee of from 1940 to 1944. During World War II, Andropov took part in partisan guerrilla activities in Finland.

In 1954, he was appointed Soviet Ambassador in Hungary and held this position during the 1956 Hungarian Revolution. Andropov played a key role in crushing the Hungarian Revolution. He convinced a reluctant Nikita Khrushchev that military intervention was necessary. In 1957, Andropov returned to Moscow from Budapest. In 1967, he was relieved of his work in the Central Committee apparatus and appointed head of the KGB . Two days after Leonid Brezhnev's

death, on November 12, 1982, Andropov was elected General Secretary of the Communist Party. During 15 months in office, Andropov dismissed 18 ministers, and 37 communist first secretaries. In August 1983 Andropov made a sensational announcement that the country was stopping all work on space-based weapons. One of his most notable acts during his short time as leader of the Soviet Union was in response to a letter from a 10-year-old American child from Maine named Samantha Smith, inviting her to the Soviet Union. Smith made friends with children in Moscow. This resulted in Smith becoming a well-known peace activist.

For the last two months of his life Andropov did not get out of bed, except when he was lifted onto a couch while his sheets were changed. He was physically finished but his mind was clear. Throughout his last days Andropov still worked, even if it meant little more than signing papers or giving his assent to his aides' proposals. On December 31, 1983 Andropov celebrated the New Year for the last time. Andropov died on February 9, 1984 in his hospital room.

Because of his short period in office, I did not receive his autograph. Adropov wrote several books. His last one was published in 1983 and he gave a copy to a Lady who worked for Hungarian communist leader János Kádár. Many years later I met the old lady and she was so kind to add the Andropov book to my collection. The book is dedicated to her name by an other hand – but signed by Andropov.

Mikhail Sergeyevich Gorbachev / 1931- /
President of the Soviet Union / 1988-1991/
Secretary-General of the Communist Party of the Soviet Union / 1985-1991/

He was the last Head of State of the Soviet Union, and father of "Glasnost," "Opennes" and "Perestroika" Restructuring. Gorbachev was born in the village of Privolnoye. He was ten years old when the Nazis invaded the Soviet Union in 1941. At age 14, Gorbachev joined the Komsomol (the Communist League of Youth) and became an active member. He joined the Communist Party in 1952. In 1978, Gorbachev, age 47, was appointed as the Secretary of Agriculture on the Central Committee of the Communist Party. By 1980, he had become the youngest member of the Politburo. After Chernenko's death he became the leader of the Soviet Union at his age 54.

Gorbachev brought a fresh new spirit to the Kremlin. Young, energetic and married to an attractive, stylish, and educated woman, he represented a new generation of Soviet leaders, free from the direct experiences of Stalin's terror which so hardened and corrupted many of his elders.

Gorbachev also sought to establish better relations with the United States, which might allow some reduction in Soviet defense spending in favor of consumer goods. In November 1985, he met with President Reagan in Geneva. The clearest signs of improving Soviet-American relations came in 1988 when Gorbachev visited Washington D.C. While Gorbachev's political initiatives were positive for freedom and democracy in the Soviet Union and its Eastern bloc allies, the economic policy of his government gradually brought the country close to disaster. On November 9, 1989, people in East Germany were suddenly allowed to cross through the Berlin Wall into West Berlin, following a peaceful protest against the country's dictatorial administration. Gorbachev, who came to be lovingly called "Gorby" in West Germany, now decided not to interfere with the process in Germany. He stated that German reunification was an internal German matter. Between August 20-22 and September 22, 1991, Estonia, Latvia, Lithuania, Ukraine, Belarus, Moldova, Georgia, Armenia, Azerbaijan, Kazakhstan, Kyrgyzstan, Uzbekistan, Tajikistan, and Turkmenistan declared their intention to leave the Soviet Union. Following his resignation and the dissolution of the Soviet Union, Gorbachev remained active in Russian politics.

His 80th birthday on March 2nd this year, has been celebrated in all the World. In February 1986 Hungarian leader Kádár paid an official visit to Gorbachev. It was the second time I asked for Kádár's help. I wrote a kind letter to Kádár, enclosing a photo showing him with Gorbachev and I asked him to sign the photo and to ask Gorbachev in Moscow to autograph the picture as well. Kádár did it, a little time later the photo was returned to me having both Kádár' and Gorbachev' signatures on it.

President Gorbachev with U.S. President Ronald Reagan

Flag of the U.S.S.R.

The Beatles: A John Lennon Signature Profile

By Stephen Koschal

It has been said that if every issue of all the magazines on autographs had a story published on the signatures of The Beatles it would not be enough. This is mainly because there is so much controversy over the autographs created by those who call themselves experts on the signatures of the Fab Four.

I have met most of the handful of so-called Beatles autograph experts here in America and I can assure you that I have become wary of any Beatles autograph that comes with their COA.

When The Beatles came to America I was just out of my teenage years. I realized the historical importance of their visit and was successful in getting a ticket for their visit to Shea Stadium in New York. Living in the New York area, I have attended many concerts but this was to be like none other.

It was August 15, 1965, and The Beatles were in Manhattan. They took a helicopter from Manhattan to Queens and arrived at Shea Stadium in a Wells Fargo armored truck. It is said that 2,000 security persons were present at this event. My seat wasn't the greatest but I had my binoculars, which helped me get a closer look at the small stage.

The Beatles came out of the locker room and ran across the field to the small stage. The entire crowd of over 55,000 fans erupted into a frenzy. The screaming was deafening. Some of the security guards covered their ears. Some fans, out of control, jumped onto the field in an attempt to reach The Beatles. None that I witnessed were successful. Nobody other than the band members, their entourage and security were allowed on the field. It seemed even those with good seats were far away from the band. However, with all the screaming during the concert, it was difficult to hear much. Even the distance of the fans from the band wasn't enough to stop the many gals and some guys from crying and some even fainting.

This was the most famous concert event of its era and set records in attendance. If you weren't a Beatles fan before attending this event, you certainly were after it was over.

Signatures of The Beatles: George Harrison, Paul McCartney, Ringo Starr, and John Lennon

Since John Lennon (1940-1980) seems to be the most popular of the foursome, this article will touch base on his signature. Lennon's signature had many changes over the years and many of the so-called experts are not aware of the various changes. One must also keep in mind that John Lennon's signature is probably the most forged of all The Beatles.

John Lennon's first book *In His Own Write* (Simon & Schuster, 1964) was very popular. It seems Lennon signed numerous copies of this book and most all the ones I have seen signed beat a genuine signature.

Cover and typical signature of John Lennon in his book *In His Own Write*

With a bit of luck, you may find one of these books not only signed but containing an original sketch by Lennon.

A year later, Lennon published his second book *A Spaniard in the Works*, however signed copies are much more difficult to obtain.

Another way of obtaining a genuine signature of John Lennon is to be patient and wait for one of his checks to appear on the market. Most of the checks are filled out by a secretary but bear a genuine signature of Lennon. There are checks issued on the District Bank Limited in London and also on the National Westminster Bank Limited in London.

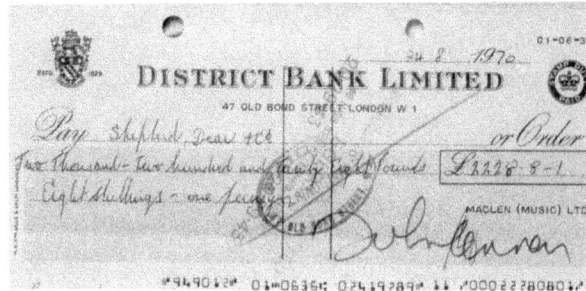

Check signed by John Lennon

Another way of obtaining a genuine signature of John Lennon iss to find a contract signed by him. Numerous contracts have appeared in the market over the years. Many of the contracts cover the distribution of royalties. Some of the contracts are even signed by all four Beatles. Contracts between Lennon and his attorney have also appeared in the market.

Contract between John Lennon, Yoko Ono and their Attorney

Signed albums are tricky and many of the self-promoting experts will disagree whether an album contains a genuine signature or not. A favorite of mine is the ultra-controversial album *Two Virgins*. Produced in 1968, this album pictures both John and Yoko Ono totally nude. An unsigned copy of the album is extremely collectible and a signed one is an absolute treasure. Several of these albums have appeared with genuine signatures of Lennon. Lennon had no objection to signing these albums and he would even sign these albums several years later. A friend of mine who is a well-known in person collector obtained one of these for me. Both Yoko and John Lennon signed the album.

A favorite amongst collectors are signatures of John Lennon when he adds his self-caricature. These very desirable self portraits of a smiling face wearing glasses are available from time to time.

Signature of John Lennon along with his trademark self portrait

My files on the signatures of The Beatles is enormous. However, if I were to invest a large sum of money for their autographs I would contact Alexander Mehl, who I consider the world's foremore expert on their signatures. Should you want to experience a modern day Beatles extravaganza, I would suggest you watch out for the next meeting of the Ada 1986, the German autograph club. They usually have the extensive full room educational display of autographs of The Beatles. The display has been created by Alexander Mehl. May I suggest that everyone interested in The Beatles signatures not miss the opportunity to enjoy this fascinating display.

Autograph of the Quarter

Qaddafi, Muammar el (1942-) President of Libya (1969-) Very scarce printed color photograph, 5'x7" head and shoulders pose, smiling. Boldly signed in green ink offering excellent contrast.............................$250.00

We offer quality autographs in all fields of collecting.
**Large Selection of World Leaders, Aviation, Political, Inventors,
Literature, Nobel Prize, Music, Sports, Hollywood, Undesirables,
Civil War and Supreme Court.
Large Selection of Signed books!**

Autograph Authentication is our Specialty.
For more info contact:

Stephen Koschal
P.O. Box 311061
Miami, FL 33231

Phone: 561-315-3622 email: skoschal@aol.com
Website: www.stephenkoschal.com

Eyewitness to the Lincoln Assassination

By Stephen Koschal

Throughout the decades letters have entered the autograph market written by those who were present Friday evening, April 14, 1865 at Ford's Theatre in Washington. They were there to see the play *Our American Cousin*.

It is rare to find a letter written by someone who was actually an actor or actress in the play.

A young actress in the play was Jeannie Gourlay.

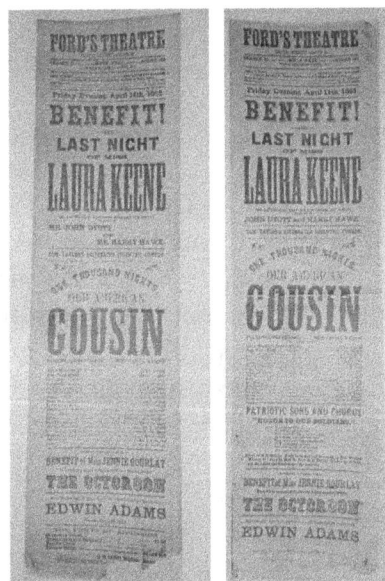

First
Issue

Second
Issue

Playbills from the night of the Lincoln Assassination

Over 20 years ago an autograph manuscript signed by Jeannie Gourlay Struthers came to the autograph market. It was her eye witness account of the assassination of Abraham Lincoln. She wrote:

"I have always thought John Booth selected a certain part of the play, Our American Cousin, in which I took part, to assassinate Abraham Lincoln, it was near 10 at night, his body guard had left the private box and was sitting in the parquette. The scene I speak of was entirely between Asa Trenchard and myself, who played Mary Meredith. When I came on the stage I saw standing in the lobby John Wilkes Booth he looked so strange I hardly knew him. We went on with the scene, I looked again and he was gone. Asa Trenchard burned a will leaving his fortune to Mary the audience are intent listening to this part of the play. I went up the stage and the scene was closed in. One of the scene shifter was Ned Spangler who was supposed to have been in the private Box that day with Booth, fixing a Bar of Wood, to place across the door to prevent any one from getting in after he was there. The leader of the orchestra and I were standing behind the scenes talking when I heard a shot, not knowing what it was, and a loud murmmer (sic) not knowing what it was and saw coming from the 1st entrance Booth, with a long knife in his hand, he slashed Mr. Withers with the knife, pushed me out of his way and went back out the back door into the alley and rode away."

Signature of Jeannie Gourlay Struthers on her eyewitness account

Thomas Gourlay, the father of Jeannie, was a part time stage manager and actor. He was also appearing in the play as Sir Edward Trenchard, an English gentleman with money problems. Thomas raced to the box where Lincoln was being attended to by doctors and actress Laura Keene. The doctors wanted Lincoln to lie on the floor and Thomas not wanting Lincoln's head to touch the floor took a 36 Star American Flag which was draped over the facade of the State box and placed the flag folded under Lincoln's head. Thomas Gourlay was one of the men who carried Lincoln across the street to the Peterson House.

Thomas Gourlay kept the American Flag as a souvenir and just before his death in 1888 gave it to his daughter Jeannie.

Well over a century later, the flag which took part in one of the most traumatic events in American history became linked to another tragic event. A thin strip of the blood stained flag which held Lincoln's head measuring 2 inches long by less than a quarter inch wide was stitched into the National 9/11 Flag recovered at the World trade center on September 11, 2001.

History is always amazing!

TheSigning.Com

. TheSigning.Com is a new autograph auction site that has been designed for buyers and sellers of autographs. Finally there's a place to go to sell and buy autographs without the fear of being kicked off because someone else doesn't believe you when you obtained the item in person. TheSigning.Com will allow you to sell autographs with very low listing fees and only a 5% final value fee TheSigning.Com has been created just for the specific needs of sellers and buyers alike where everyone is invited It will allow you to easily list items or bid on items with built in features that have been created just for the autograph industry. If your just buying, the site will allow you to surf through thousands of listing that have been broken down into specific categories. TheSigning.Com will feature current news and blogs related only to the autograph hobby. TheSigning.Com will not be contaminated by outside influences that have destroyed the selling or buying ability of highly reputable sellers on other sites. This site is not controlled by outside influence's with conflict's of interests. It is the one place where all buyer's and seller's can participate.

www.TheSigning.Com

Piece OF THE PAST, INC.

Experience the Difference Authenticity Makes!

Piece of the Past, Inc. is pleased to announce the official launch of its new online auction site! Housed at www.pieceofthepast.com, this site replaces most, if not all, of our eBay sales activity as well as our monthly catalogs.

You may be wondering why we'd make this move. The answer is simple. We want our customers to have the very best experience when adding to their autograph and/or memorabilia collections, and by controlling all of the aspects of the auction process, you're guaranteed to receive the best service at always fair prices.

The site is up and running right now with an array of fabulous photos, costumes, and props, so the follow the directions below and join us now. You won't be disappointed!

Registration Instructions

1 - Go to http://www.pieceofthepast.com

2 - Click the button that says CLICK HERE TO REGISTER

3 - Enter your name, address, phone number, and other information

4 - You will receive an e-mail confirming your registration and assigning a bidder number. That is your permanent number.

5 - Log into your account and start shopping!

6 - Check back often because we'll be listing roughly 200 items per week.

9030 West Sahara Avenue, Suite 448 - Las Vegas, NV 89117 - (888) 689-7079

Choose a city to attend the Hollywood Show.

Burbank/LA
Four Times Per Year!

NEXT SHOW:
February 10-12, 2012

Las Vegas
Twice Per Year!

NEXT SHOW:
May TBA

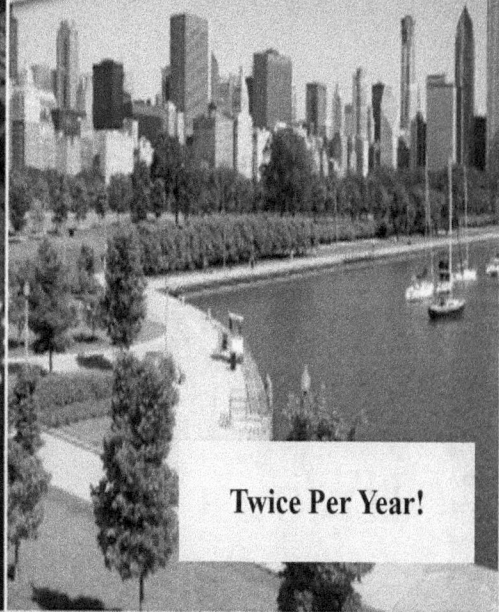

Chicago
Twice Per Year!

NEXT SHOW:
March 24-25, 2012